COMPUTER SCRIBBLES

Project Management

It's More Than You
(Or PMI) Might Think

Dana Kilcrease, PMP®

Also By Dana Kilcrease

A Time Of Essence
A Renewal Of The Heart Most Timely

*For those who realize that boundaries are meant
to be crossed.*

Table Of Contents

A Note About Footnotes

There are lots of footnotes in this book. Normal writers use them for making references to other publications, or to clarify points which are too obtuse for regular people to understand with their puny little brains, or to include all those *ibids* and semi-colons and other literary delights which are oh so academic but in reality are fully and totally uninteresting. This, not being a normal book, does not use footnotes for these traditional purposes. Instead, they are used to make snarky comments and puerile jokes that don't fit neatly into the flow of what I'm writing at the time. Of course, those could be more entertaining than the text itself, which is why you should read them. But, being what they are, footnotes are typically ignored, as so much extra fluff that doesn't contribute to the *book* itself. To which I say: balderdash. Please be sure to read the footnotes.

(Heck, if you've made the effort to actually read the book, you might as well get some entertainment value out of it.) (Hey! That could have been a footnote!)[1]

---

[1] And *that* could have been one, too!

The best laid plans of mice and men often go awry[2].

- *Robert Burns (1785)*

---

[2] The original Scottish version of this is somewhat less comprehensible to today's contemporary English speaker, but is still quite lyrical:

The best laid schemes o' Mice an' Men, / Gang aft agley.

From "To A Mouse, On Turning Her Up In Her Nest With The Plough", by Robert Burns.

Preface

Since this book tends to be written from an IT perspective, it might be said that I'm an IT guy, and that's somewhat true. Actually, I'm a business value guy. There are many different layers of value when discussing *technology*, and I've been involved in all of them at one time or another. There are many different layers dealing with *business value*, too, and everything in between. Of course, to a client, the business value layers are the most important, because that's what their company is all about. Technology, to the client, is a necessary evil, and only exists to provide support for the *important* things that actually run the company and produce revenue. Technology is a (huge) expense, which therefore detracts from their bottom line. And, anyway, it's getting more and more commoditized every day, which makes it *so* hard to distinguish between individual technology vendors.

Especially for those "decision makers" who know precisely zip about silicon.

Those technology vendors, though, think of things a little differently. Their company (indeed, their entire corporate life) is totally wrapped up in delivering *this* technology to *that* client (who just sniffs at it with raised nose). Because, of course, delivering that technology product is *their* business value. And the technology vendor depends on their own ecosystem of suppliers, each of which has their own value stream to worry about. And on and on. The end result is a massively complicated web of interdependent and interwoven supply chains that forces every company to end up in bed with one another to astonishingly complicated degrees.

When I say that I'm a business value guy, what I mean is that, when I work with a client, I take their perspective about what's important. I know technology isn't. Oh, it's interesting and cool and *tres chic* when you're talking about something business people think they understand, like their iPhone. And it's true that part of a consultant's role is often to lead the client's technology decision toward a favored vendor. But the reality is that no one on the side of the company who pays for the technology actually understands it. And no matter how polite they are when they say they do, they *do not* care about it. Sorry, Bub.

Here's a true story to illustrate that. At one time, I was working for a company that built computers. I was lucky enough (seriously) to go out on a customer visit, to a power company in the mid-west who was having problems with our brand-new system we'd just sold to them. When I got there, I found out that the system had been having such severe problems that the company had literally backed a truck up to their loading dock to yank it out. The customer said to me "Look, you have to realize that the only reason why I have your system in here is because it happens to run the application I need to manage my power generation environment. If the system is unreliable, I can't run this power plant, and that's bad for business *and* my career. If it breaks again, you're out of here, and I'm putting your competitor's system in to replace yours." Luckily, a service update had arrived the night before, and that stabilized the system to the point where the customer eventually kept it.

That, folks, was my indoctrination to what *business value* is really all about. It didn't matter that the customer had our system powered from the same circuit that drove their coal supply conveyor belt, which drew more amps than Cleveland. All that mattered was that the system had to work so they could run their power plant, and it didn't.

But, technology does have a good place in a book like this, too, because it's so easily quantifiable into boxes and widgets. That makes for very easy examples when explaining a point. It's much easier to talk about how long it takes to build a server, and how expensive that is, and how many people it takes to do the work, and what the procurement cycle is for that, and so on, than it is to talk about re-engineering a business process to be more efficient and measuring that. So, for this book, I tend to stick with tangible and well-contained widgets to make points.

But this doesn't mean that the concepts of project management don't apply to other areas. They certainly do. In fact, struggling with understanding what work has to be done, who will do it, how much it will cost, and when it has to be done, can be applied to essentially any endeavor you undertake. Think about it. You want to buy a new puppy? Hmmm... once you figure out what kind to buy, you have to decide who's going to clean up after it, and how long that would take. And, how much does the vet cost for those ridiculous shots? And all that puppy chow... yikes. Believe me, puppies are a project unto themselves. A delightful one, to be sure. But the point is that you can apply the concepts of project management to literally anything and everything, including getting a puppy.

On a more, well... *sophisticated* level, though, a project can deal with renovating a kitchen, buying a company, writing an iPhone app, building an airplane, or dumping your girlfriend[3]. OK, or boyfriend. So, that isn't very sophisticated. But it does take a lot of time. And it can get really, *really* expensive. And lots and lots of people can get involved. (Lawyers, BFFs, come to mind.) You get the point.

And speaking of points... one of the things I do in this book is to emphasize points, by, well, emphasizing them, so you'll remember them. Like this:

Major CS+PM Point: *If it looks like a project, and swims like a project, and quacks like a project... it's a project.*

If we dissect that, the first thing to observe is the bullet heading: **Major CS+PM Point**. I think that's kind of self-explanatory. But, for the managers among us, you'll note the **bold** font, and the word "**Major**" to indicate that something important is happening. "**CS+PM**" is, of course, the short-hand acronym for this book. And "**Point**" lets you know that a point is being made. Clever, isn't it? And all that is followed by (ta dah!) the point itself, in all its glory.

---

[3] Ahhhh... I'm not going there. Too many opportunity costs. And pain points.

So... at this point, so to speak, I think you've had enough preparation to read this book. There are some very good people, across many industries, who have worked diligently for years and years to codify what "project management" means, and how to go about doing it. But even with those big brains, they don't always capture the salient points about the pragmatics of the discipline, at the point of the spear, in the trenches, where the rubber meets the road, the tip of the iceberg, the... OK, enough clichés. I hope this book helps you see what it really means to be a project manager. It can be a very fulfilling career, though at times it seems to have more than its share of frustrations. And as a PM, *you* have to overcome them. It's not all wine and roses. It tends more toward beer, I think...

Enjoy.

Introduction

When you start a new job, it takes a while to get over the feeling of being the Gladiator fighting the hungry lions in the Coliseum, which can take a week, or a month, or most often, seemingly forever. The reality is that, however long it takes, you won't feel comfortable with the environment you've just dropped yourself into for some period of time. You'll eventually get to the point where you delude yourself into thinking that you know things, like how to use the tools there, what the organizational protocols are, and how to work with all the different kinds of people you've been meeting. You start to think that, just maybe, you aren't the sacrificial lamb any more, and you really do understand how things are done there. And then - *uh oh*, you realize that, heck, it isn't that you're finally getting to be a productive member of the team there. No no, you've merely just learned enough so that you start to understand *how much you don't know*.

What I mean by that is this...

Major CS+PM Point: *Newbies make lots of mistakes. Your success as a Project Manager depends on how quickly you can recover from them, and how soon you can stop making them. And that takes time, which you don't have a lot of, and some practical guidance, which this book provides.*

There are things you need to know in order to succeed as a project manager. The chapters in this book are organized to provide some insight into the numerous perspectives you need to develop along the way. There is a precedence order at work with them, which is more important in the early chapters. But don't worry too much about that. Instead, just focus on sipping at the trough of experience here, and letting these concepts and ideas meld into your new knowledge base as you read through the book.

Here are the key chapters...

What's the point of this book? - A level set about the underlying philosophies of the book, and what's truly real.

What IS "Project Management"? - A practical discussion about the discipline of project management, written from a perspective borne of experience, and without all the normal boring blather you find in all those other books.

Bullet 1: Discipline Expertise - Yes, you have to know the nuts and bolts of what "project management" is all about, but you need to know what else is involved, too. And it's those extra things that make your work so ... interesting[4].

Bullet 2: Domain Expertise - You need to know about the area you're building a project for? Who knew?

Bullet 3: Leadership - Don't go thinking this is the last thing you need to know about, but be real clear in understanding that this is absolutely the most important thing you need. Nothing else will work without it.

Socialism - You think politics aren't part of project management? Ha!

---

[4] There's a saying, which is supposedly a Chinese curse: *May you live in interesting times.* Just a little apropos to project management.

Faith - Oh, yes, when there are so many unknowns flying around, you need lots and lots of faith that you can pull things together.

ManageMental - Unfortunately, you need to deal with management when managing projects, so a tutorial about these types is called for.

Requirements - Do you know what you're doing? I mean, do you *really*? No, you don't. Here's why.

PMeontology - noun, [*pee-em-ee-on-tol-oj-ee*] (from English *Project Manager*, "a person with a lot of *wisdom*, a.k.a. years under the belt" + Greek *ontos*, "the study of"); <u>Definition</u>: the study of high tech fossils; <u>Synonyms</u>: obsolete (*contemporary*), big shot with lots of worthwhile smarts (*prehistoric*)

Decrankification - How to be less cranky about what the future holds for you as a Project Manager.

What's the point of this book?

My name is Dana Kilcrease.

Not a good opening line for a book, you say? Why would I say that, when you already know my name from the book's cover, or the internet, or from a zillion other places? (OK, maybe not a whole *zillion*...)

I said that because I want to make a point about it. Which is this:

My first name is "Dana". Not "Dan". Not "Donna". It's DANA.

But that isn't the point.

It's fairly common that when I email someone, we've never met, so they have no idea who I am. All they know is what I write in my email.

Emails typically go like this:

"Dear XYZ Company, can you please send me some great information about your new product, Yippie Ki-Yay. Thanks. Dana Kilcrease."

And they respond like this:

"Dear Ms. Kilcrease, here's a link to our website where all the information you want is located. Thank you. Customer Service."

See that? "Dear Ms. Kilcrease..."? *MS*.?

It just so happens that the term "Ms." doesn't apply to me. Not that there's anything especially wrong with the term. It's just that I happen to be a GUY, not a GAL. So, I'm not a "Ms.".

I've gone through my entire life having to deal with this misperception. Sometimes, it's just sloppy systems implementation. I used to run technical seminars for something called "data analytics". This is when data is analyzed to ferret out information that data relationships can indicate. (Kind of like what the NSA is doing to your email *right now*.) Normally, this is used to look at business things, like sales transactions or web clickstreams, to develop marketing campaigns which are targeted at individual users depending on their purchase or web history. But sometimes this gets a little off track. I used to get catalogs in the (snail) mail from various companies. Some would send a catalog to me, addressed to "Dana Kilcrease". That's goodness, since that's my name. But the same company would send me

ANOTHER copy of the exact same catalog, but address it to "Dana L. Kilcrease, Jr.". Yes, that's a more complete form of my name. But that's bad, because catalogs are expensive to produce, and I only need one, not two. (I don't really need ONE, actually, for the kind of useless stuff they put in them...) But then the same company would send me yet ANOTHER copy of that catalog, and address it to "Ms. Dana L. Kilcrease, Jr." You'd think that if they go through the trouble to find out my name and address, they'd be smart enough to do some more work to figure out that there really aren't 3 people living at the same address with almost the same name. And having "MS." and "JR." in the name should be a clue about the name not being valid. Someone wrote a gender assumption algorithm that had a big fail in it.[5]

But, I digress.

To continue... If you happened to actually see me, you'd have to go a long way to mistake me for a female. But if you've never seen me, then you have

---

[5] There is a function in business data analytics which prevents this. It's called "householding", which is where the company applies some more smarts to their algorithms so that their calculated number of people living in the same household, or at the same address, is optimized to as close to the actual number of residents as possible. This saves on the costs of producing catalogs, and also saves the company from looking even more stupid than they already do for selling the junk they put in these dumb catalogs.

to make some kind of assumption about my gender when you reply to something like an email from me, because it's proper business etiquette to use a salutation and include the addressee's title in that. According to our dear Emily Post, "When writing to a woman you don't know, you can address her as 'Ms.' For unisex names like Pat, Jan, Leslie, Alex, Hillary, and Lynn, however, (Ed note: or DANA) a phone inquiry to a recipient's firm to confirm his or her gender will save potential embarrassment."[6] I love the part about a phone inquiry. Who does that? I mean, really? Does Emily really think some poor overworked, outsourced customer service type on the other side of the world is going to actually call you up to find out your gender? Hardly. But what is certain is that in today's fast-paced world, there's no time to worry about things like the gender of someone who emailed you, when there are 10,000 more emails in your inbox that you have to respond to, too.

So what people need to do is to make some kind of snap judgment about a person's gender when they respond to them. You can just leave the person's name out altogether, but it's a marketing best practice to establish a personal bond with the person you're communicating with, so that the person will be more likely to like you and want to associate with you in the future and therefore think of you and your

---

[6] See the actual hysterical reference at
http://www.emilypost.com/on-the-job/clients-customers-vendors-or-contractors/784-effective-business-letters. "Ms.", indeed.

product set when they want to buy their next widget. Or some such MBA nonsense. Thus... "Ms.".

Actually, the person making a gender assumption is more likely to be right than wrong when they assume "Dana" is a female. I looked this up on the Internet a while back, so it must be true: it turns out that 80 percent of people named "Dana" in the US are female. (Of course, 14 percent of people can prove anything with statistics, according to the famous philosopher, Homer Simpson.) That puts the guys named "Dana" at somewhat of a disadvantage when assuming their gender, but the numbers are what they are. I mean, as a customer service rep, if you only piss off 20 percent of the people you communicate with, you're pretty much ahead of the game, anyway.

Even when someone sees me, it's obvious that I'm not a female, but they still have a hard time digesting the fact that I'm named with a girl's name[7]. And that gets worse in a medium where there are no other clues about a person's gender, like emails. To help people remember my name AND my gender, I used to tell them that I'm named "Dana" just like Dana Andrews. But then people would say "Who?"

---

[7] True story: there's this one local store in my area (and I won't mention that it sells wine). I get PROOFED there. Not because I look like I'm under 21, of course, even when you're talking in dog years. No no, when I hand my credit card to the Millennial types on the cash registers, they think (to use a term loosely as applied to them) "Hey, no way can a GUY be named DANA. He must have filched his wife's credit card." No joke. It gets bad enough to drive you to drink. Which is why I go to that store in the first place. And I get proofed. Which is how we get into "recursion".

because Andrews was a film star in the 1940s and died in 1992. So I had to change my reference to someone more contemporary, and I chose Dana Carvey. But, he's so passé these days. No one remembers him from his "Church Lady" skits on Saturday Night Live any more. No one who does web programming, anyway, because they weren't even *born* when he did those things. Maybe some of the old mainframe guys still remember him. But, anyway, I have to find someone a little younger for the web kiddies to relate to.

But I still haven't made my point yet. And it isn't that I've been handicapped with a girl's name my whole life. I love my name. My father was named Dana, and my great uncle was, too. And my wife made me name our first son Dana, so it's kind of a family thing now. (Which our son has promised to end when the time comes.)

And all this is a long and silly way to finally get to the point I wanted to make, which is this:

Major CS+PM Point: *Things aren't always what they appear to be, especially when it comes to defining what "project management" is.*

OK, I'm not original with that. You may have heard the saying "You can't judge a book by its cover". THAT was original. But it's the same thing.

This is why I called this book what I did. Just like you may THINK that I'm a girl when you hear my name, you may THINK you know what you're talking about when you say you're a Project Manager. But the reality is that *your* meaning of what a "project manager" is might be entirely different from what a person you SAY that to *thinks* it means. At least, that's the case 87 percent of the time. (Which I just made up.)

Here's the deal: there's so much confusion about what a "project manager" is these days, that the *industry* had to make up a definition for it, so that everyone could agree on it. So, over a very long period of time, and after many, many discussions and beer-fueled conferences, an organization was formed to be the keeper of the flame for project management, and to define not only what a "project manager" is, but what a project manager actually *does*. And that organization was creatively named *The Project Management Institute*[8]. Or, "PMI", as we acronym-obsessed techies like to call it.

And, yea verily, in order to anoint the warriors most qualified to be project managers with a title known far and wide, so as to indicate to the world that they are, indeed, worthy of respect and hiring, PMI came up with the assignation of *Project*

---

[8] OK, OK, I know there were a lot of things that happened before PMI that led to its existence. PERT charts and Gantt charts and the Critical Path Method and all that happy stuff were all around a long time before PMI. Other books deal with that history, and the assumption here is that either the reader already knows about all that, or doesn't care. My money is on the second choice.

Manager Professional, or PMP, which in the manner of business cynicism, immediately transformed into "pimp".

Therefore, by the authority granted to me by PMI, I will forever be known as Dana Kilcrease, PMP. At least until I forget to recertify.

Good.

Now, what do we mean when we say we're a "project manager"? We could take the easy way out of that and just say that a project manager is *someone who manages projects*, and then go out for a couple of cold ones to celebrate. But, even project management isn't *that* superficial.

The problem is that every organization has a different definition of what a "project manager" is, because they all have differing viewpoints about what "projects" are, and how they should be managed.

Sometimes, an organization will extract just a small portion of what a project manager role is, and call that a "project manager" position, when it really isn't. Suppose, for example, an organization decided to take "project coordination" and define a project manager position as doing only that. We know that there are five phases (or "Process Groups" in the new terminology) to project management, and while coordinating the various parts of a project plan that are all moving at once is a PM responsibility, there's a lot more to being a PM than just coordinating things. Heck, if that's all a PM did, we could just get automated calendars and let *them* coordinate things, and do away with the PM altogether.

So, why would an organization take only one part of what a PM does and call *just that portion* a full PM position? The simple explanation is that the HR person who defined the position had no clue about what a PM actually does, so they made it up. That happens more often than you might think.

But a more common reason why this happens is because the HR person really *does* know what a PM position entails, and intentionally restricts the responsibilities of the role to justify a lower salary while still calling the position a "project manager". Cost cutting has its own special reality.

The other side of that, though, is that the HR person might stuff all kinds of PM responsibilities into a job description, and then call that a "project coordinator" job. Why do that? For the same reason: to justify a lower salary, in this case by lowering the position *title*, while at the same time including every regular PM responsibility they can think of anyway. Their hope is to get a qualified PM in the job, but not have to pay the person at a PM rate. Embrace the suck.

And there are all kinds of games played with titles of PM positions, just to keep the uninitiated confused and unable to negotiate a salary commensurate with the responsibilities of a particular job. There are the hierarchical PM positions, such as PM I, PM II, and PM III. The difference between them is exactly... what? Or, if you don't like numerology in your PM soup, there are titles like Project Coordinator, Associate PM, just plain PM, or Senior PM. And if you want to get really hoity-toity about it, there are Project Director, Project Executive, and probably Project Poobah, too. And the problem gets so bad that if a company needs a group of PMs, there has to be a separate department named for them. And it's called a PMO, or Project Management Office. And, if you catch the short straw and have to actually manage it, you get to be called the Manager of the PMO. Otherwise, you'd be the Project Manager Manager, which sounds like something out of Catch-22, which is an entirely appropriate context when discussing project management.

The point in all this falderal is that every organization has its own definition of what "project management" is, and what a "project manager" position entails, and what the pay scale for that is. Its hard to transport any of that from one company to another. So, when you interview for a job, you really need to dig into what that company means by "project management" and "project manager" so that you know how to put a price tag on the position you're applying for. Don't get caught committing to a pay rate until you know what the job is really about, and that it's something you can live with.

And, even once you get into that great new job called "project manager", you may end up finding out that the organization looks at a "project manager" as something entirely different from what they said it was during the interview. All too often, a PM position is ultimately viewed as a low-level administrative job, not a leadership position. It's a step up from an administrative assistant position, and not a large one. That, of course, is bogus. But the expectation can be that you won't be leading architectural or process discussions, or contributing any real competency to the position. Mostly, you'll just coordinate calendars (where are those automated calendars when you need them?) and get people to agree on what the plan needs to look like. This is due to a poor business culture in that group, because a project manager *is* a leadership position. And this perception will persist unless *you* do something to change it. Sure, most likely you won't have a lot of latitude in this because an organizational strategy is already in place, complete with the requisite tools and processes that are in vogue that day, and your project is probably scoped so that it fits into that and supports it all nice and neatly[9]. But if your ~~ass~~ job is

---

[9] Wine helps to get you to the point where you actually *believe* that.

on the line, you need to take ownership of every detail of that project. No matter what the organization thinks your job might be, you need to be proactive enough to own the activities in your project to the point where you can drive them to completion, through the members of your project team. A project manager position requires that you be assertive, and forward-thinking, and unafraid to use plain talk with people to get them to do their jobs. It's not that they don't want to do their jobs. (Well... sometimes it is, but not generally.) The thing is that you need to "help" them set their work priorities so that your project items can be completed when they need to be.

What this all means is this...

Major CS+PM Point: *Wallflowers don't make good project managers.*

This isn't a New York City type of in-your-face thing[10]. It's all about leadership. And, in order to lead effectively, you need to know what it is that you're leading. Since every organization looks at project management differently, even with PMI or another standardization framework as a basis, you still need to have a solid notion in mind about what *you* think project management is, so you know how to lead

---

[10] Fuhgeddaboudit.

your team, and how to set expectations with them. And more important, set expectations *with your management*. Certainly, don't be contentious about things, but don't be wishy-washy, either. You lead from strength, not from volume.

A very, very, *very* important point here is that you build a whole universe of project management in your head as you move through your career. You tweak it and tune it and keep it updated as you find out which things work and which don't. This is your knowledge base, which forms your potential value as a PM, and differentiates you from everyone else. You bring this into every job you hold, and use it to define *to yourself* what "project management" really is, no matter what the organization you're working in *says* it is. You meld these perspectives and skills with the context of your organization. The art of doing this successfully is being able to leverage this experience in the ways that your organization needs project management done, *whether it knows it or not*, while all the while being a thought leader for them in what it means to manage projects. Even if your group has a rigorous project management methodology in place, it still needs interpretation, and your mental PM universe can provide the lens for that. You add tangible value, not conflict. Remember...

Major CS+PM Point: *Project management is what <u>you</u> make it out to be as a project manager. If you don't define what it is, according to your perspectives and experiences, someone else will do it for you. And you'll have to live with that, right or wrong.*

Rah, rah! It sounds so easy. But, life tends more toward complexity, especially a PM's. What this book does is help you understand what extra little bits of pragmatism there are for you to include in that cranial universe, and how to leverage it for your best, most realistic benefit.

What IS "Project Management"?

Let's get down to it.

What IS project management?

Easy. Project Management is (wait for it...) *managing projects*.

Ta dah! Thanks for playing. C U L8R.

OK, let's restart here...

Lots of people ask you what "project management" is, because they have no idea what it means when you tell them that's what you do for a living. Including, by the way, your manager, and also lots of other project managers, who are really just asking you about that so they can compare notes and see if they're doing things correctly. Which, no, they aren't.

Let me tackle this from my standard IT perspective. Suppose you're part of a large organization. Here's what that might look like:

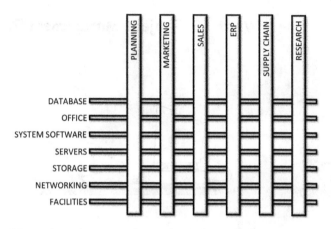

Note that there are lots of bars in this - some running vertically, and some running horizontally. The vertical bars are the business towers, pretty much application areas. The horizontal bars are the infrastructure areas, all the things that have to be in place to support the towers. It all looks so nice and neat, right? Sure, on "paper" it does.

Now, let's take a look at what the problem with this is...

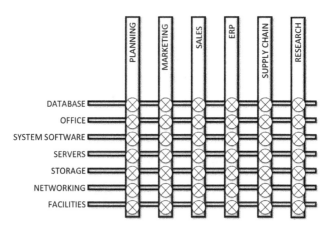

 = POINT OF RESOURCE CONTENTION

See all those little circles with Xs in them? Those are organizational points where resource conflicts happen. This graphic might look two-dimensional, but really, it represents a many-to-many set of relationships between the horizontal areas and the verticals. Every single vertical tower needs some amount of resources from every single infrastructure area. Why is that?

Look at Marketing as an example. What does Marketing do[11]? Suppose they want to put out a marketing campaign for one of their spiffy new products. They have this list of customer names, like in the thousands. That's not real handy to keep on little pieces of paper floating around your desk. So

---

[11] Go ahead and answer THAT one. PLEASE.

you put them into some kind of tool that lets you manage and work with them. That's a database. But, even if you get the database software for free, which you won't, a database isn't "free", because it takes up system space. So, Marketing also needs storage to hold this database. Now, to actually DO something with the names in the database, Marketing needs some kind of software that provides a "campaign development" set of functions. That has to live someplace, too, so more storage is needed. But, it can't actually run in storage, so it needs some server time. This application also has to be able to send out spam emails to all the customers on the names list, and it does that through the network, which means there's some incremental new network load that's required. And the various marketeers who are working together in the corporate dungeon to put this campaign together have to communicate with each other as they do their nefarious plotting, which means they need some office app to coordinate their precious calendars and let them whine to each other through emails. And, finally, all this technology stuff doesn't just wander by when you need it. It all has to live someplace, too, and that means you have to crawl to the facilities folks to get some floor space for the new servers and storage devices, and electricity to run them, and lights and heat and... so on.

So, Marketing puts a request together for all this good stuff to support their new marketing campaign, and throws that over the technology wall for the infrastructure teams to provide. Nice.

All that works great for just one group. But there are other groups who also need servers and storage and networking and software and facilities, too, and a whole lot of other things. So, if you're some poor schmuck in, say, the storage area, you have this huge list of requests for more storage space from all the vertical groups. And of course they aren't actually offering *funding* for this space. And they all need the space *right now*. So you have to figure how to provide all these storage spaces to all the requesters and then pay for it all and hide that cost in your allocation that you charge back to these requesters and then make sure it gets done right away so you don't have to work over the weekend to do it. Which you will, anyway. And overnight, too.

But, hey, life can't really be that simple. And, it isn't. Why not? Because you can provide all the great storage you want to, and it won't do any good if the server time isn't provided *at the same time*, since the applications have to run on the servers in order to process the data in storage. So you have to somehow coordinate all the storage requests with all the requests for more server time because they go hand in hand. And the new network capacity needs to be in place for the same reason, too, and the software, and every last little bit across the whole infrastructure. And, oh, yeah, to do this, you have to work across five data centers with about 7,000 servers and all the things that link to them, like your storage. And *UPS* likes to talk about "logistics[12]".

What your organization has is a crying need to coordinate all these requests that are flying all over creation so that they all get done at the right time, while making sure that there's money to pay for them all, and people in place to implement them all, and your technical people don't just explode from sheer joy. Or something.

And, I know, I know, Cloud will fix all this happy horse puckey. But, only for paying customers, who will be paying a LOT for the privilege of handing over their entire technology environment to some specious Cloudie. If you happen to be a Cloud provider, though, you've bought yourself an entire universe of this kind of technology management nightmare. Why else do you think that companies want to unload that?

Now the question becomes, how can anyone in their right mind manage this insanity? Ah... insanity... what a great segue back to project management.

---

[12] Well, they can, because they're particularly good at it.

Let's take a look at what "projects" look like relative to resource requests.

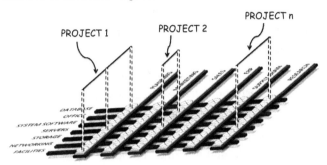

PMI defines a "project" as "a temporary endeavor undertaken to create a unique product, service, or result[13]". It then goes on to define "project management as "the application of knowledge, skills, tools, and techniques to project activities to meet the project requirements." OK, cool.

When you boil this down, what it means is that a "project" requests resources from some number of the horizontal areas, and maybe some of the vertical areas, too, to implement a piece of work they need done. In this graphic, *Project 1* could be the implementation of a new application that does strategic forecasting. This application needs more

---

[13] From the PMI PMBOK (pronounced "PIM BOK"), or Project Management Body Of Knowledge. I know, some people actually think a PMBOK is a type of herding animal found on the Plains of Serengeti.

database space, more server time, and some facilities space to expand into. To figure all that out, a group of smart people needs to get together and brainstorm about this, to put all the new functions which are needed onto "paper", and to work with the technical architects to see how that expands into new servers and space to hold them. It's a left-to-right process - first identifying what needs to be done, then figuring out what it would look like, and who would implement it, and how much it would cost, and when it can be completed.

Project 2 could be a smaller effort that Sales needs, perhaps to put better spellchecking into their sales plan because they keep getting confused about quotas and such. That, yes, is a cheap shot, and I take it right back[14]. But, if that project were to happen, it would need more capabilities in the front end of their Office application, and some server time, too.

Ah, there's an illustrative point... both projects need more server time. What is the poor server team to do?

But, wait, there's more!

There's another project in the works, called *Project n*. Why is it called the "nth" project, when it's the one after the second project? Because it's not really the project that comes after the second project.

---

[14] No, I don't.

Project n represents a continuing stream of projects that flow out indefinitely, ad infinitum[15]. There is another project on the horizon after the first two, and another, and another, and... well, so on. The point here is that there are an infinite set of project requirements coming from the vertical towers, and sometimes from within the horizontal infrastructure, too. And these infinite requirements all have to be implemented using very finite horizontal resources.

There's an actual formula[16] which represents this:

Major CS+PM Point: *Infinite requirements + finite resources = organizational contention*

Now, no one likes contention. But organizations are set up intentionally *to be contentious*. Why?

Suppose you're in charge of setting up a business organization. Part of doing that is to provide a set of business capabilities which can be used to operate the business. The purpose of operating a profit-making business is normally to generate profit[17]. Profit is good. (*Greed* is not, no matter what Wall Street

---

[15] Or ad nauseum, your pick.

[16] Which I just made up. I LOVE writing.

[17] A profound thought there. You'd think some of the Internet companies would recognize this. Maybe someone should tell them. Twitter, you listening?

says.) Profit is what really makes the world go 'round. The two parts of "profit" are *revenue* and *cost*. The point of a business is to maximize revenue, and minimize cost, so it can take home as much profit as possible. When it comes to implementing a business capability, such as a sales system, that capability represents direct or indirect revenue generation. But the implementation of that capability isn't free. Nor is the operation of that capability. Both cost *something*. The more it costs, the less revenue can be realized as profit. So, a business wants to keep costs as low as possible.

Sad to say, technology doesn't generate revenue (unless that's what you're selling). Sales folks out in the field pestering potential customers to buy their products drive revenue. They may use internal systems to record their sales and send out bills and deposit their measly little commissions into their bank accounts, but those are all costs of supporting the sales process. The cost of sales is subtracted from the revenue of sales to arrive at a profit figure for sales. The company may decide to improve their internal systems so that they're more efficient, and technology can certainly play a role in that. For instance, the company could buy new technology to replace the old technology so that the systems run faster or can handle more transactions. But that's expensive, which means it's a significant cost. So, they want to keep from doing that unless it's absolutely critical.

People are expensive, too, so a business will hire as few people as possible to keep from going belly up. Cutesy little MBA techniques like "outsourcing" and "layoffs[18]" keep direct hires, and hence personnel costs, to a minimum.

The net of all this is that costs are minimized by keeping investments in things like technology and people and facilities as low as humanly possible. Or, lower.

When you originally set out to design this business, you could have chosen to set up an implementation group which could handle any sort of request essentially instantly. That would be, of course, exorbitantly expensive, and there goes your profit. And, probably, your job. So, you want to bring the costs down a little, which means you buy a little less technology, and hire fewer people to run it. And, as a result, your implementation group doesn't cost as much, but it has to take a little longer to actually deliver these critical business capabilities. But, meh, no big deal. And then you decide that, heck, you can squeeze a little more profit out of this thing by turning the screws on your implementation group just a teensy bit more, and you lay off a few people which

---

[18] Funny how those two things go hand in hand.

you think will save you a couple of shekels. But, the group's delivery time is getting a little longer now as a result. Oh, and the quality of what they deliver is suffering some, too. Doggone programmers. But, you like what you see, so you do it again. And again.

Now you realize that your competition is getting more intense, and you have to do something to beat that. So, you ask your implementation team for more business capabilities, hoping against hope that they can keep you from losing more revenue, and can maintain your very thin profit margins. But of course, you can't afford to expand your implementation group, because investing in that would just mean risking more sunk costs in the future, and who needs that aggravation. So, you load up requirements on your implementation group, and tell them to "buck up", for the good of the company. And they take even longer to get things done.

What you're doing is putting more and more requirements onto your implementation group, which has less and less ability to deliver them because you can only get so much blood out of a rock. Eventually, your group will no longer be able to deliver the requirements you need because there are just too many of them. And when they can't deliver the business capabilities you need, you fall further and further behind in the marketplace, and eventually you realize that your company is going down for the count, and is taking your golden parachute with it. You have jumped onto the death spiral of "cost management". Thank you, B-school newbies. Penny wise, pound foolish.

To avoid all that negativity, you put a management system in place to handle the unending requests coming into your implementation group. And that management system is administered from on high by the *Project Management Council*, an omnipotent and coffee-spilling group which meets every *week*, and is composed of management types who have tee times coming up.

Now, a problem standing in your way is that the implementation team has only so many arms and legs, which means they can get only so much work done in any given time period. So, if there are 10 projects which all need storage space, well, then, these projects will just have to line up and *wait* for their requirements to get completed. Sorry. Go tell it to management for deciding to "manage" costs on the storage team. Of course, if one of those projects at the back of the storage line happens to be yours, you can always go to the all-powerful Project Management Council and cry to them about why your requirements should be given a higher priority than everyone else's. But, the people on the Council have been there and back, and they've heard lots of whining which was *all* better than yours. So, you end up just having to wait.

Infinite requirements, levied against finite resources. Which rhymes with "C" and that stands for "CONTENTION". OK, so it doesn't rhyme. Sue me.

The overall point in all this is that there has to be a balance in an organization between the things which need to get done, and the costs of doing those things. And since there are always more things to do than there are people to do them, there is contention in the organization for those people. And this is done by design, to manage costs.

But this is where project management comes in. See,

Major CS+PM Point: *Project management is meant to help identify and manage requests for organizational resources.*

We've said that project management happens within the context of a project. But, an organization can have lots and lot of projects going on at once, all competing for the few resources in place to deliver things. So, a management system needs to be put in place to instill some degree of rational order to this. And that *system* is "project management", too. If there are multiple related projects all going on at once, that forms a "program" hierarchy. So, sometimes this management system is called "program management", and the people who are doing this work are "program managers". Fine. I've been a project manager, and a program manager. And I've managed project managers, and program managers. Honestly, the distinction between "projects" and "programs" is one of semantics, not practicality.

I say this because at times, as a project manager, I've managed multiple related projects at the same time. In fact, not to toot my own horn here, but there have been times in my career that as a project manager, I've managed over 25 projects concurrently[19]. By standard definitions, that would make me a "program manager". OK, whatever flicks your Bic. But there have been other times, too, when as a "program manager", I've managed just one project. It all depends on how the particular organization you're in views these things.

So, when someone asks you what "project management" is, you have a whole series of perspectives to answer with. In fact, you can fit your answer into whatever reality you want to. Why?

Because the problem with the question is that it isn't *real*. People don't ask that in real life. Oh, your

---

[19] And you wonder why most of my hair is gone now! OK, that's mostly from our kids, but project management is a reason for that, too.

wife or husband might, just to be nice at dinner one night, or if they're having a hard time falling asleep. Why? Because this is the type of subject that makes people's eyes glaze over. I think the record for that happening is less than a half second.

This is the kind of question you hear in job interviews when the interviewer, who is NEVER a project manager, wants to see how you respond to tough questions. Like, this is a tough question. To him it is, sure. But to you, Sir Knight of the Round PMs, it's a cakewalk. And you answer by rattling off the first things that pop into your head, and then wonder, "who the heck said THAT?"

I heard this question once in an interview at an international high tech company. The Director I was interviewing with said this:

"Imagine that you have to make a presentation to a large group of people, and the presentation is about project management. You have to explain what it takes to be an effective project manager, in just one chart. And the chart can have only 4 bullet points on it. Tell me, what are those 4 bullet points?"

In retrospect, this was actually a pretty good question. And of course, I answered it with things that came to mind right at that instant. I never knew the Yankees were involved in project management before.

But since that interview, I've had a lot of time to think his question through. And I realize now what mistakes I made in answering it, the first one being this statement: "Hey, I can do that in only 3 bullets!"

I actually said that.

OK, not quite exactly like that. Here's the thing... you don't want to go changing the requirements from the customer right off the bat. It takes a while to shape their heads. This Director had already told me that the requirement was to list 4 bullet points, not 3. But, sometimes, you have to push the envelope.

In my mind, all this time later, this is what I would have said in response:[20]

"That's an interesting question. I really think there are 3 points to make here, though, which are these:

Major CS+PM Point: *To be an effective project manager, you need to have these skills:*

1.   Discipline expertise
2.   Domain expertise, and
3.   Leadership.

---

[20] Which means that, no, I didn't *actually* say these things. What I *did* say is thankfully lost to posterity now. But as to your next question, no, I didn't get the job. Their loss.

And the Director would have said "But I asked for 4 points." And then you would have to backpedal a little. But, let's ignore that part for now.

Let's imagine, since we're imagining anyway, that the Director said "Ah, that's interesting. OK, tell me what each point means." And that's when I would have gone into my "what I did with project management over my summer vacation" spiel.

Bullet 1: Discipline Expertise

The first thing you need is discipline expertise. I say "expertise" here instead of "skill" because I want to be difficult. No, no, I say it because "skill" is too granular. Learning to do only one little, tiny thing is a skill. An expertise, however, is an entire portfolio of interrelated skills, that all mesh perfectly together to make you into a true expert in your field because you can do all manner of great things. I grant you that "a true expert" might be a little overly optimistic... but the point is that when you have an "expertise", you really are good at something that takes a lot of different skills to do.

What do I mean by that? Well, for instance, I play golf. It takes a lot of skills to play golf. Note that I didn't say, play golf "well". That is something not in my vocabulary. But, I do love to play the game, and it does take a lot of individual skills to play it.

Like, you have to be able to hold your beer.

And you think I'm kidding! That's the first rule of golf.

But, seriously, to play golf, you have to be able to do things like, oh... put a golf ball on a tee without it falling off. Now, you might not think this is much of a skill, but remember, a skill is just a small thing you can do, and if you can't tee the ball up, you can't hit it. There IS a precedence order at work here. And remember the beer factor, too.

Then, another skill you need is to be able to swing your club at the ball[21] and be able to hold on to the club with enough strength so that it doesn't go flying out of your hands and into the woods. To follow your ball after you hit it, presumably. Another valuable skill.

And once you actually succeed in hitting the ball, you need to have good enough visual coordination so that you can watch it as it wends its way through the trees, thereby knowing where it lands after it bounces off some large number of branches and squirrels and such.

Hopefully, you don't need to hit the ball over some inconsiderate water, because you don't want to employ your breath holding skills that let you retrieve

---

[21] And actually hit it. Minor point.

your ball from the pond quite yet. Better to save that for the back nine.

See how I play golf?

But, back to project management... if you listen to the experts (a.k.a, PMI) about what the project management "methodology" is, you'll hear things like this: it's a waterfall process that includes the five phases of project management, from initiation all the way through closure, all of which are wrapped around this thing called "the triple constraint". This might sound like we're heading toward an S&M discussion, but fear not. Let me give you a little background on this.

I've been a project manager since before that was an industry-wide regimen called "project management". I know, that sounds like a stone age kind of thing to say, and technologically speaking, it is. But way back in the dark ages, before there was this magical mystery tour called "the internet", there was a huge monolith called "programming", which was worshipped by large groups of hairy mathematicians at sunrise every day. Unbelievably, we had to do things then that are still done today, though we didn't go about it as religiously as today's practitioners do. Sometimes, and I know this might sound fantastical, we actually started out a programming effort by speaking with other people so that we could understand what work needed to be done. Now, the surprising part of that statement could be either "speaking with other people" OR "understand what work needed to be done". The reason why people became programmers was because they didn't want to speak with anyone else. And that kind of defeated the idea of knowing what work needed to be done before we started doing it. But, that being said, we did do that. Sometimes.

Once we got into the midst of the actual programming, we found that there were lots of shiny objects there to distract us. And distract us they did. Why, for instance, would I ever want to code something that some other person would want to use? I mean, isn't that the same thing as me doing *his* work? Why can't he do his own work? No thanks, I'm keeping my subroutine library to myself, if it's all the same to you.

Or, what do you mean you need this program on Wednesday? No way! I haven't figured out how it needs to speak to the other dozen or so programs in the system already. I need at least until next week to get it to you. What do you mean, the Vice President[22] wants to see it tomorrow? Who said that? What's HE care about this?

Or, why did your program trample all over MY data? *Yes*, it's my data. I generated it. And your

---

[22] Let's call that what it really is... the President of Vice.

program doesn't even know how to use it. What do you mean, the data's not correct? Sure it is. I told you about it yesterday. And I only made a couple of changes in it since then. Can't you keep up?

You laugh.

But there are a few universal enlightenments which can be drawn from this. Hence, I call this "The Project Manager's Path To Enlightenment":

1. You can't do any work before you get the blessing of the management team (including people like this VP).

2. Before you start to do work, you need to know what work needs to be done. (This is the "*Duh* Rule".)

3. You need to know when the work needs to be completed. I mean, unless this is for the government, work can't just stretch on to infinity.

4. When the work is going on, you need to involve everyone else in it so that they know what's being done, too.

5. You can't just change things whenever you want to. You have to involve everyone on the team in any decisions to change something, so that they know what's being changed, and so they can figure out what changes they need to make in THEIR work to

accommodate the silly things you want to change.

Why is all this stuff important? Simple - because:

Major CS+PM Point: *If you don't follow the PM's Path To Enlightenment, then you WILL need to do a bunch of YOUR work over again.*

This is called "rework", which is a dirty word in business, because doing something even once is expensive enough, and having to do it over again because you screwed something up is doubly expensive[23]. Or more. Minor things like *your career* can be affected by this kind of thing.

So, is this the clarion call that will convince you to never become a programmer? Not by a long shot.

This example might be about a set of programming problems, but the same things can happen anywhere. Business, science, relationships, you name it. Anywhere. You are surrounded.

Just think about it... in anything you do, that *thing* takes work. If it doesn't take work, then it doesn't exist. *Worko, ergo existo*. Work is tangible, and for all you spreadsheet jockeys out there, it's quantifiable, too. You define *work* to be a set of

---

[23] Rework is a bitch.

things which need to be done, and then you have to figure out how many people you need to actually do the work, because there's no way you could do it all yourself even if you HADN'T let your technical skills erode so badly. And then you have to figure out how long everyone will take to get it all done[24]. And then you have to do all the math to figure out how much all this will cost. And that's when you get into all the stupid politics that come into play any time real money is involved, and you have to deflect all the asinine questions from management about that. Like, "This takes 4 months to do? Hey, I need it next month. Give me a good schedule for a change, would you? And no, you can't have Larry to work on this. He's doing important stuff." Or, "Who said you could do THAT? Hell's Bells, that isn't what I wanted. Go rework this piece of $#!+ you call a plan and get me something I actually want." Dale Carnegie would be *so* proud.

But in all this, I think you can start to sense a pattern emerging. There are a certain number of things you need to do to get a glob of work done, and it doesn't matter what that glob is, really. And every time you get a new glob of work to do, you have to do the same things for that glob as you did for the

---

[24] Don't forget to factor in all the whine time your team will ask for. "Oh, I can't do it in just a week. I need a whole month. Waaaa." Like that.

previous glob. And so on. You just have to repeat the kinds of things you've already done for any new glob[25] that comes your way.

And you end up writing down all the steps you take, because who can remember all that stuff? And you tweak it and tune it and eventually end up with a list of things you get to do anytime you have to do work. That's called a *process*. Actually, the purpose of defining a process is so that you'll know what you need to do the NEXT time you have to do some work. And this process isn't only about YOU. It's about everyone on your TEAM, so they ALL know what they have to do to get the work done. Isn't that nice? And it isn't just about THEM, either. It's about ALL of you. Together. Working as a TEAM. KUM BA YAH!

And here's a silly thing... it's not just a *process* that you do over and over and over, which is what a process is *for* -- to know how to do something over and over and over. It's sometimes called a process that you *repeat* over and over and over. Or, a *repeatable process*. Isn't that repetitively redundant? Didn't Einstein say something about insanity being when you do something over and over again and

---

[25] Isn't "glob" a great word? No, it's not an acronym. It's just something that popped into my head as I was writing this. Sounds like something out of "The Twilight Zone". But the meaning of the word is pretty obvious. It means... "a glob". You're welcome.

expect different results? So, *process* is institutionalized insanity. A logical conclusion I can buy into.

Anyway... the problem with all this is that your process is for your team only. Suppose you need to work with another team to get your work done. Shouldn't they use the same process you do? Of course they should! If they only knew about it, I'm sure they would, and happily. But they don't know about it. So you call a meeting with them, and stock up on lots of programming health food (e.g., coffee and donuts), and have a talk. And they agree to use your process. But, they want to make a couple of "minor" changes to it, so they can have a codified way of poking a stick in your eye when you're late on delivering something to them. OK, you agree to that, because you can use the same process change on *them*, if need be. And, the result is that you have a great process for your team and their team.

But, now you find out you have to work with 3 other teams to get the work done, too. You can't just go and negotiate with all 3 of them about changes *they* want to make to the process. Who's got that kind of time? *Tick tick tick*, time is money. So you decide to publish a process that works for everyone, and have a regular meeting to talk about how it's working. You just *standardized* your process, at least among your small group of teams.

But more teams hear about your process, and fall in love with it. And so you let them in on your secrets, and they start using your process, too. But they ALL want to make some more minor "changes" to it, and before you know it, you have this huge conclave of teams that you have to manage every month, and they all end up throwing food at each other. Now, now, kiddies...

This is kind of what happened in past efforts to standardize processes to get work done. Everyone had their own view about what steps needed to be included, and who needed to do what, and on and on. It was pretty close to industrial anarchy.

Until, that is, a group of dedicated people got together and decided to work across all the various business industries to come up with a process that everyone could agree on and would use. And so, "project management" was born. And the organization that gave birth to it (eventually, anyway) was PMI.

And the process PMI developed was called the PMI Project Methodology. This methodology defines how you start a project and get executive sponsorship, which means the execs tell you what work to do and how little they'll agree to pay for it to be done[26]. And how you figure out how many good

---

[26] There's never enough funding. Never. Never ever ever.

people need to work on it, and for how long. And how to actually set the pace for execution of all the various work items. And how to dip your toe into the water of the project every so often so you know how things are going, and how to fix things when they break. And they will always break. And, finally, how to wrap things up and show everyone how great a project manager you were during all of these trying times.

Now, a lot of people see this type of *process* discussion, and it's hard for them to keep their heads from exploding. Why? Because they haven't gotten their little handsies burned by not having a process in place when they needed to get some work done. See, it's all too easy to think, "Ah, I can just slap this thing together in an hour, I don't want to get too *formal* about it." They view process as a waste of time. They're professionals, real experts. The lead goose in the formation, and all that. They show the way for everyone else. So, why do they need a process to get things done?

I've seen instances where a very small group of true experts actually did do a phenomenal amount of work in a very short period of time, and didn't use a "process". In one case, two people wrote code at ten times the normal rate for their organization. They completely rewrote a major office application in almost no time at all. How could they do that?

They locked themselves in a room and didn't come out until it was done. That is a literal statement. OK, coffee runs and nature breaks (which go hand in hand), reintroducing themselves to the little people at home once in a while, and the infernal STATUS MEETINGS, are all aside. But it was just the two of them, and no one else, who was involved in the actual development work.

Let me ask... how often does something like this come along?

Answer: never.

And the point is...

Major CS+PM Point: *For any project effort today, you can't do it all alone. If you could, it wouldn't be a project.*

You always have to work with someone else to get the job done. That means you have to depend on them to get some work done for you, and you have to do the same for them. Any time you have a dependency on someone else, you have to agree on what they need from you, and what they'll actually deliver to you, and when it all has to be done. Goodness gracious, you have to put an actual *plan* in place for the work. Then, probably, you have to take that plan to eight different levels of management to get them to agree on it, so you need to remember to put enough extra time in your plan to accommodate all those dunderheads.

But, there are never just the two of you doing the work, are there? No, no. If the work is actually worth doing (always a matter of perspective) then there will be lots and lots of little pieces of work that need to get done, and *so many* people you'll have to work with because each person will need to do their own little, teensy piece of work. And all those pieces of work all have to be coordinated together, so they get done on time.

And that, my friends, is what you have to know cold if you want to be an effective project manager. Why? Because you need to know what parts of the process to use, what parts to throw out, what parts to change, and how to defend all that to your management, who most likely don't know beans about project management and don't really care. But you need to know it all.

So, great. Now you know what "Discipline Expertise" is. That's all you need to know to be effective, right?

No?

Of course not!

The only reason why you made it into project management was because you had some superior level of *Domain Expertise*.

Say what?

Bullet 2: Domain Expertise

I've heard it said that if you have good management skills, you can manage anything. Doesn't matter if it's a programming effort, or a financial services implementation, or building a data center. If you know how to manage, you can manage anything.

Baloney.

Here's the point...

My wife is a teacher. When she says to someone else, "I'm a teacher", the other person is bound by law to say "Oh, what do you teach"?

See, being a teacher means that you know how to teach, sure. But there's more to it than just that, so you have to clarify your statement. You teach, but you teach *what*? And in this case, teach *who*? It isn't enough to just be a teacher. You have to teach a particular subject to a specific age group of students.

The same is true for a project manager. You tell someone you're a project manager, and it's like "Come on, man, don't leave me hanging. You're a project manager, but of *what*?"

Just like being a teacher, being a project manager means you have a veneer of skills, in this case management skills, that you can apply to *something*. That bears repeating:

Major CS+PM Point: *Being a project manager means you have a very thin veneer of management skills that you can apply to something.*

But, apply these skills to what? THAT is the question. To PM, or not to PM.

I love the antacid ad on TV that shows a doctor trying to use a jackhammer. Here's this skinny little bald-headed guy in a white lab coat, trying to hang on to this massive jackhammer while it bounces all over creation. And this burly construction worker is looking at that, in rapt wonderment. Then, a deep, resonant voice says "You wouldn't want your doctor to do your job. So why are you trying to do his?"

Believe it or not, project management is like that. Yes, you do have to use a jackhammer on some people.

NO. Don't try that at home. Just kidding!

The point that many project managers miss is that when you manage a project, you actually have to know something about the thing you're managing.

Rude awakening, isn't it?

But it makes sense. How, for instance, can you manage a project to develop a software thingie if you don't know anything about programming? Or, how can you manage a construction project when you couldn't even handle your Legos as a kid? Heaven forbid that you try to manage a project to build a new device for doctors to use if you don't even know how to spell "M.D.".

The point here is that you need to know how to take all your good project management skills that go into your PMP, and be able to apply those skills to doing that special something with the things you're trying to build. For instance, I've managed projects to build out data centers. First of all, I had to know what a "data center" was. You may find this hard to believe, but some people think you're talking about a logical location in the data. You know, its "center". I sure don't want any of *them* managing my next data center project.

But to build a data center, you have to know things like what a "server" is, and what "power" is, and what "air conditioning" is, and so on. And you have to know what "water seepage" and "floor loading" and "fire suppression" are. And lots of other tasty things. You don't get that knowledge overnight. You have to build it for years and years, to the point where you actually know about it. And only THEN can you apply your wonderful project management skills to it and have a meaningful outcome.

See, this all makes logical sense:

Major CS+PM point: *To manage a project which delivers X, you need to know what X is.*

So, what does having all this great skill about "X" do for you? Well... you can use all that great stuff to get into project management. Of course! How? Well, suppose you grew up in a technical role, like being a system admin. And you're getting to the point where you know so much about what needs to be done in that particular area that your company figures you might be able to tell *other* people what to do, and you coerce them into making you a *team lead*. The problem with that is that then you can't do as many of the technical things that you're really good at because you have to do all the handholding and diaper changing for the people on your team. But, what the heck, you probably got a minuscule pay bump in the process, anyway. And, the more time you spend leading your team, the more you realize that you might as well get better recognition for it, and you decide to get your PM certification because you're already doing most of the stuff PMs do, like putting schedules together and figuring out how to get your team to stop playing Solitaire and do some work for a change. Good. Light and nourishment await you along your chosen odyssey.

Or, you may end up following the dark path, where the company likes what you do so much as a team lead that they decide to put a full stop to your technical growth, and they mount you on the Ultimate Pedestal of Impending Obsolescence by making you a department manager. The problem with that, aside from the abject joy you get from giving people performance reviews right before laying them off, is that you absolutely *will* get to the point where your skills are so eroded that when you finally wash out of management, which comes to all management types sooner or later, you have no base of actual skills you can fall back on, and the only thing you remember how to do is tell other people what to do. So, you figure that, hey, you can be a "project manager", because that's all *they* do, at least the ones *you've* seen. Tell everyone else what to do, and then listen to them *whine to the execs* about how your project is falling behind schedule. Again. Heck, piece of cake, you can do *that*. And you get your PM certification as a fail-safe mechanism to your dwindling career.

Ah, well... yes, that was pretty much sarcasm[27]. But, the point here is that you can grow into being a project manager through either the technical path, or the management path. There are lots of ways to get to be a PM, and no way is better than another. But, you really do have to know something, by which I mean *a lot*, about the area you're going into as a PM.

Having said that... don't be surprised when management says, "Hey, you know what the 'World Wide Web' is, right? Great! How about managing this project to build a healthcare portal for the entire country? Sure, you can handle it. Heck, you know what the 'web' is, don't you?"

I have visions of pointy haired managers running around in my head right now.

Here's something to remember as you ponder what planet people like that come from: no one knows everything about *anything*.

That's why you work in teams. You pull people onto your team who actually know about something. Like, cartography. (Which, no, isn't drawing pictures of carts.) You're building a GPS app, so you need

---

[27] But not entirely. You're "chosen" to become a manager in an area because you were good in the domain of that area. But being a manager takes an entirely different skill set than what made you good in that area to begin with. Not everyone is cut out to be a manager. Not even smart people. (HA HA, funny guy.)

someone on the team who actually knows about maps. What an idea, right?

The thing is that you build teams to do more than just supply (hopefully) breathing bodies[28] to do work. Sure, more bodies, more work. But you build teams so you can get people involved who actually know what they're doing. You need to install a new application? You get an admin for that application on your team. You need to design a new flower shop? You get an architect on the team. You need to do a specific thing on your project, you get an expert in that thing on your team. Why? Because they know what needs to be done. Phew.

What I'm saying here is that, as a project manager, you don't need to know how to do every single thing on the project. You need to know who *does* know these things, though, and then know how to conscript them onto your team. That takes good skills to negotiate with their management, because every organization is always short on competent people, and so the ones they have get pulled in a bazillion different ways every day. So, what you need to be able to do is to understand the work well enough so that you can pull the *right* people together

---

[28] A manager type actually said this to me recently. He was telling me about how a group was staffing up and they "need bodies", and would I be interested? So I said, well, I DO have a body... but, no thanks.

who can do the actual work, and you can work with them to create the plan to pull all this off. Or... out... of *someplace*... depending on your perspective. On time, under budget, and all that other gorpy stuff.

So, the important thing here is this: when you are assigned a project[29], the person who gifts this puppy to you makes the radical assumption that you actually know something about the area, or "domain", the project addresses. (That same person also spends half his income on lottery tickets.) But, it does make sense, if it were true. You don't want to run a project to migrate a network if you don't know what a "network" actually is. Right?

OK, let's get back to reality here. You already know that organizations are short of people these days, because the economy is in the tank and companies aren't making their financial numbers and costs have to be "managed". The standard company line. Of course, "managing costs" is just a cutesy little euphemism for saying "we will be cutting your salary and hours and will probably give your job to some fine mercenary type from way far away. Love and Kisses, Company CEO." Gotta love the power of the dollar.

---

[29] Or, more likely, when you *inherit* a project from some other project manager who has decided to chuck his career and run off to write the Great American Novel. About project management, of course...

Anyway... because organizations are chronically short of bodies, they put their people into a large barrel and spin them around like crazy. Then, when a project needs staffing, some poor resource manager type reaches in to the barrel and pulls someone out, and slaps a sticker with the name of their role on their forehead, and throws them into the cage where the next project is being done. Whether or not you get pulled out of the barrel to be a project manager for an area that you have actually *heard* of is random chance. I call this "PM Roulette". But the same holds true for any skill set. When your number's up, it's up.

So, you, the great data center PM, bring all your great data center skills into your new project. Which, by the way, happens to be designing a new milking machine. And you know exactly *what* about milking machines? Well, nothing, of course. So why did the resource person stick you on this project? Because you had "Des Moines" on your resume, and that's farm country, and anyone who's ever been in farm county knows about milking cows. Obviously.

I kid thee not.

And like the good soldier that you are, and also because you want to keep your job, you decide to go ahead and see if you can muddle [30]your way through the project, by hoping you can pick up a farmboy

---

[30] Better known as "fake".

along the way who has actually seen a milking machine. You know, a milking machine *architect*. I imagine those kinds of people actually exist. They have to, or else we wouldn't have milking machines[31]. And they all live in Des Moines. Obviously.

I keep nudging around this "reality" thing. The scenario I'm blathering on about here isn't really that far off from what you might see in reality. Organizations really are short of people, and people really are asked to take on assignments that might not be an optimal fit with their skill set and background. (Nice way to put that, isn't it?) So, if you're a victim of PM Roulette, you may find yourself leading a project where you, well... have some blank spots, let's say. You typically won't get onto a project where you have absolutely NO background whatsoever in the domain. But you could well be put on a project where your fit is, for lack of a better phrase... kind of light. Does this mean you just fold your tent up and go home? Nay nay nay. All you have to realize is that the person who put you on this

---

[31] I had dinner once with a client who was from a major paper company. His job was to design toilet paper. Seriously! He described all the various aspects of what needed to be considered when doing the design. Such great dinner conversation. But that was his WORLD. And he LOVED it. And we need people like him. Because, can you imagine what things would be like if no one was around to design your toilet paper?

project knows even LESS about milking machines than YOU do. So, you are all geared for success. It's unavoidable, actually. No?

Well... no. In fact, the odds of succeeding are pretty much stacked against you. "But," you say, "I know all about project management, and I know every last detail about milking machines, so what else could I possibly need?"

And then a voice someplace in a hidden and underused wrinkle of your brain whispers "You need *leadership*".

Hearing voices, are you? Believe me, before you're done with your journey into deepest, darkest PMville, you will hear LOTS of voices.

Bullet 3: Leadership

There are two metaphors for project management which help illustrate the abject hopelessness of the discipline: plate spinning and juggling. I can, of course, do neither one. But juggling doesn't quite demonstrate the point here. See, when you juggle, you throw things (like tennis balls, razor sharp knives, sticks on fire, running chainsaws, kittens[32]... take your pick) into the air, and then catch them when they fall back down so that you can throw them back into the air again. The theory is that when you do this, you won't end up catching the thing in the wrong way, and end up slicing off a finger or three. Or self-immolate. And project management is a target-rich environment for self-immolation.

---

[32] NO, don't use kittens. Gads. And no dwarves, either.

But the problem with the juggling metaphor is that the event of catching a ball and throwing it back into the air is too transient. The reality is that when you catch something as a PM, that thing tends to stick to you like glue, and it's next to impossible to get rid of it quickly. This is the project management "rule of anti-deflection". And if you drop the thing you're juggling, you know it right away. There's no suspense. What fun is that?

Spinning plates, though, is the perfect way to depict what project management is really all about. There was a guy on the Ed Sullivan show way back when in the age of dinosaurs and black and white TV who used to do this plate spinning act. He'd take a plate and put it on top of a real tall, skinny wood stick, and spin the plate like crazy so it would be stable enough to stay up there without falling off. You could always tell when a plate was starting to slow down its spinning enough to be in danger of falling off the stick, because it started to wobble. And when that happened, the guy would run over to the stick and yank it around in circles to get the plate spinning again. And, he wouldn't do this with just one plate -- he'd have a whole row of these things going, all at once. So, there was all this suspense about how many plates he could keep spinning without any of them falling off their sticks.

Well, that was the theory. This was way before we had PlayStations to keep us entertained.

Anyway... how does this relate to project management?

Easy. See, you're given something to get done, which is represented by the plate. And you have to get the thing spinning on this ridiculously tall and skinny stick, which represents the set of conflicting and precarious constraints like under-allotted time and funding and resources that you deal with every day on a project. And once you get this plate spinning, you have to leave it alone while you're off doing something else, because you've been given another plate and you have to put that on top of a stick and spin it, too. Then you have to repeat this same foolishness with yet another plate that you were given, and another, and another. What you end up with is a bunch of plates spinning merrily along, perched on their sticks.

But (and here's the kicker that makes this a better metaphor than juggling) you come to a point where what you see is a whole row of plates spinning on these tall sticks. And they are all spinning along just fine on their own, thank you very much. So you stand back, and admire your work, and start thinking that, hey, things are really going pretty well. And you kind of forget that the plates are actually spinning a little slower and slower all the time, because they haven't slowed down enough to start to wobble yet. And you develop this kind of naive, ignorant *hope* that, heck, since things are going so swimmingly right now, they'll continue to do that *forever*.

And then reality rears its ugly head into your dreamy little vision, and a plate starts to wobble. So, you run over to it, and yank the stick around enough to get it spinning again. And you notice that another plate is starting to wobble, and you have to run over to *it* and get it spinning again. And then you see that three other plates are starting to wobble *all at once*. And you try like crazy to get them spinning again. And then, in your worst plate spinning nightmare, one plate falls off its stick. And it crashes into the stick next to it, which knocks that plate off, and *it* crashes into the stick next to it, knocking *that* plate off, and on and on, until all the plates are lying on the floor in broken pieces.

And the most painful part of this is that, at one time, you had a glimmer of *hope* that things were actually going to work out well. And that hope gets dashed into little pieces, at the worst possible time, in a way that makes fixing it essentially impossible, which reminds you of what a lost cause hope can be.

Yes, indeed, the comparison to project management is quite clear.

What's the point of all this? It's this...

Major CS+PM point: *No matter how good your plan is, there is always room for things to go wrong[33]. And they will.*

Your job at this point, and the thing you have to do to survive as a project manager, is to not just *find* all the broken pieces of your plan, which is tough enough, but you have to be able to pick them all up, and get your whizzbang plan glue out, and patch all the parts back together again into something resembling a workable plan. Or, one that you can at least sell to management as workable. For some period of time. Whatever.

But *survival* and *succeeding* are not one and the same. You can survive a plan crisis by glueing things back together when they break, and can then limp along to the next crisis, and hope (there's that word again) that you'll have enough plan glue to put your Humpty Dumpty plan back together again when it breaks the next time. And the next time. And the

---

[33] I have to give credit where credit is due on this one. In my early years, I worked with a wonderful man whom I will call Heath T. Heath was an excellent programmer, with an insightful sense of humor and irony. He had a multitude of terrific expressions about things. One time, when he was reading over some code, things just didn't look right to him, but he couldn't spot the specific problem. So, he said "I think there's room for a bug in here someplace." His intuition was right on, of course, because there was a bug in the code, as we found later on. I shamelessly, and with thanks to Heath, paraphrase this saying of his.

next. But the fallacy with this is that eventually, and this is a locked-and-loaded guarantee, you will hit a crisis that is bigger than you are and you can't fix it, and you better have your flame-proof underwear on when you go tell management about it. Because you will get mightily singed by this.

So, *survive* is not what you want to do. Yes, I know that survival is a career strategy in today's floundering technology market. All this hooey in the media about how great the job market in high tech is makes for nice reading if you like fiction. But, the fact is that the overall tech market is depressed (as are most people in it) because the economy sucks, and consumers aren't buying things with the wanton disregard for the future like they used to, so companies have huge inventories they can't sell, and that makes capital investments in things like technology not smart. This all creates a tremendous amount of turbulence in the job market, because more and more people are looking for fewer and fewer jobs. And they are *all* more qualified for that job you want than *you* are. So you have to do a lot of scrambling to stay employed. And that leads to you just trying to survive from day to day so you can keep food on the table and beer[34] in the fridge and make

---

[34] GOOD beer. Craft beer from micros. Not that light beer piss. Who drinks that stuff? You might as well save your body the

your payments on that spiffy new Boxster out in your driveway that you leased in a weak moment when coming home from a bachelor party one day.

Ain't life grand?

No, it's not survival that you want. What you want is to be able to anticipate problems before they happen, and put plans in place to avoid them, and when they happen anyway (which they will) be able to minimize them and keep them from growing into a Death Star aimed right at your nose. And why is that so important? Let's be honest here. The only thing that management cares about is results. They don't care about all these silly little problems (car accidents come to mind, or when your best admin defects to another company) that crop up from time to time and ruin your oh-so-nicely-crafted plan. No, no. You have a job to do, and if you can't do it like you *said* you would, well... let's just say that no one is indispensable. Got it? It's a cold, cold world.

In PMese, this is called "risk management". There are all kinds of risks that are just lying in wait for you, ready to drop a sinkhole in your path that will swallow you up for ever and ever. Amen. There are high-level risks that are really beyond your control (like your company going belly up) but that can still

---

trouble of processing it and just pour it straight into the commode. But then even your septic tank would complain.

fall on you with the weight of Zeus. There are mid-level risks (like your Director getting "disengaged" with your project because he's too busy kissing up to his VP) and you can't get the help you need to get your plan back on track. And there are the low-level risks, at least in the eyes of management, that you have to deal with every day, and no one really cares to hear about. Things like, oh... a server blows up and your best admin has to go rebuild the stupid thing before the client comes unglued, just because they actually want the business to *keep on running* (imagine that) and that takes your guy away from the project work you had planned, and your schedule gets stretched until it starts creaking like a rubber band right before it snaps.

Here's the deal: forget about the high-level risks. They can affect you, but you can't affect them. There isn't a contingency plan on the face of this or any other planet you can put in place that could mitigate that kind of damage. If you happen to be in the wrong place at the wrong time and the sky drops on your head, tough noogies, tell it to the hand, nothing to see here, move along.

The mid-level risks are more interesting, mostly because you're pretty much just an observer. Sometimes, you get to sit back and watch things break apart, and someone else (more senior than you, obviously, because *everyone* is more senior than you are) will jump into the breach and heroize themselves to get things fixed up. You may have a sense of schadenfreude[35] about this, but that's just an ephemeral glitch in your hormones, because you *will* get dragged into this at some point. The better course of action for you is to preemptively raise your hand and volunteer to help *solve the problem*. Gosh, what a great team player you are! Way to suck up. Primo stuff.

It's the low-level risks that will get you. Why? Because a) you have to fix them, and b) no one else wants to hear about them, so you can't get any reputational leverage out of them. They're like fire ants crawling all over you, biting and stinging you in the most private of places, distracting you from *real work*, making your life even more miserable than it

---

[35] This is truly one of the great words of all time. Thank you, Germany. It means you get the pleasure of watching someone else get spanked, just for your own personal entertainment, with no impact to you at all. Or, so you hope. (Don't worry, when the "mud", as it were, starts flying, there's always enough to go around.) I think of it this way: suppose my dog decides to poop on the rug. Again. The natural outcome of that is a "discussion" between me and the dog about the various merits, or demerits, of soiling my very expensive rug. Now, while this is all going on, the cat happens to be sitting in the hallway, watching this exchange gleefully, and soaking it all in. *Oh, doggie was bad again*, she thinks to herself in her tiny little cat brain. *Ha ha on doggie*. Kitty is experiencing the schadenfreude of the situation. Our neighbors, however, are probably reaching for the phone to call Animal Control. The situation is decidedly NOT schadenfreude for them.

normally is, all while you're running back and forth keeping the metaphorical PM plates spinning. This is the famous "churn" that you've heard about. Things percolate in this little punchbowl of a project you're "managing", and sometimes, the percolation bubbles over the side of the bowl and makes a mess on the table. And it's up to you, and you alone, to clean it up.

The biggest low-level risk is that some number of the critical resources (a.k.a., "people") on your team will get yanked off your project to go fix a production problem. Why? Because people have (at least) 2 jobs: their project job, and their real job. A project job is planning and developing and testing and putting all the teensy little pieces of work together to form a "solution". It can be any of a whole variety of things, like a technology implementation, or upgrading an application, or reengineering your finance process, and so on. But the point here is that none of this "project" is in production yet, so it can't really hurt the company if it decides to puke on itself. But all the previous projects ARE in production, which means the business is actually running on them now, and so there's a huge dependency on keeping them working so that the company stays afloat. If something in production breaks, it has to be fixed. Pronto. But if something in a project breaks... meh. It has to be fixed, sure. But the company won't go under because of it. Your *career* may go under if the breakage is significant enough. Or frequent enough. So as the PM, you have some urgency to get it fixed. But that's nothing compared to the urgency the *company* feels to get a production problem fixed.

And the sad fact of life in the world of project management is that something in production is always breaking, and your project people are always getting taken away from doing their project work to go fix it. Always.

Well, you say, we have ways to handle that, right? Just put some more contingency into the plan to account for people getting kidnapped to fix production problems. And then you realize that "contingency" is just another way to say "stretch the project timeline waaaaaay out", and you know that won't fly with management.

"But, wait," you say. You negotiated with the manager of the person's group that his availability to this project would be 40 percent of his time. And that was a solid commitment! How can he not honor that?

"Honor"? In project management? Oh, too funny!

Remember back to the discussion about what project management really is, and how an organization has horizontal and vertical groups that intersect and contend for limited resources, and how project management can be the integration system where you manage all that. *That*, my friends, is a good theory. But this is where the *art* of being an effective project manager separates from the *mechanics* of project management.

Here's what I mean by that...

Suppose you like music. Further suppose that you really like piano music. You like it so much that you want to learn how to play the piano. You know this will take a lot of time and effort to accomplish, but what the heck, you can find some spare time to do it because you're a PM, and PMs have lots of spare time. (Ha.) And you read about the piano, and music theory, and waste lots of that plentiful spare time on the self-teaching courses you find in the nooks and crannies of the Internet, and finally realize that you really need to get some lessons from a pro. So, you find a blue-haired granny piano teacher who has a huge ruler to smack your knuckles with when you miss a note[36], and after some number of years of suffering her ministrations, you can actually play the piano. In fact, you can play the piano so well that you become a concert pianist. And you play your favorite piano piece, Gershwin's *Rhapsody in Blue*, at Carnegie Hall.

Hey, if you're going to dream, dream big.

------

[36] And you thought the nuns at St. Mary's Elementary were bad!

But, the reviews come in for your concert, and you're disappointed to read that your music was fine, but had no *feeling* to it. Every note you played, every single one, was exactly correct. It had the right pitch, of course, because you made sure the piano was tuned before the concert. And every note had the exact right duration. And every note was spaced exactly correctly from the note preceding it. But, the music came across as flat, because there was no *emotion* in your playing.

So, you get a recording of Gershwin actually playing the piece, and you memorize every single inflection he used, every intonation, every pianissimo and fortissimo and every other musical dynamic he used. You finally get to the point where you can play the piece exactly as he did.

And the reviews come in from your next concert, and you read that you've made some improvements, but your playing sounds like a hollow imitation of Gershwin, with no originality. Yucko.

The problem is this... you've spent all this time learning to play the piece from studying the sheet music, which is by nature an imperfect and mechanical interpretation of the music. You've gotten quite good at it, but it's still mechanical, like midi-music.

Then, you learned how to imitate Gershwin exactly, and you got so you could play the piece just like he did. Certainly, that's an accomplishment, but it's still not very original, because you're just replicating how he played. There's nothing of *you* in it.

What you've done is teach yourself how to be a musical *impersonator*, where you can learn to play music like the composer did.

The thing is that you spent all this time and effort so that you can play someone else's music, but you aren't writing your own. You're an impersonator, not a *composer*. And it's in the composition of the music that the real craft of music, and the art, happens.

When you're an impersonator, you *follow*.

When you're a composer, you *lead*.

See, an impersonator can only imitate what someone else created some time ago. But the composer has moved beyond that now, and is creating something new, for new groups of others to imitate.

Not everyone is born to be a composer. You might think it takes a certain amount of "hardness" to be a leader, but that's not true. What it takes is focus and perseverance, rare commodities out in the real world. You don't have to be a hardass to be a leader. In fact, those kinds of people tend to flame out pretty quickly, and we are thankful for *that*. But, hey, we need followers, too. You've heard the expression that "there are too many chefs in the kitchen". Someone has to be the top dog. And let's not be squishy about it, others have to follow along and do what they're supposed to do. And they are *happy* to do that. If you present it to them in the right light...

You know, you might think you're a leader, but as Bob Dylan said, "you're gonna have to serve *somebody*". Life is relative. To one person, you may be a leader. To someone else, you may be a follower. What matters is what you believe about yourself.

Major CS+PM point: *In project management, you want to be the composer, because that's where leadership is.*

You don't want to sit back and be passive about things. Problems? Ah, I'll fix them when they happen. What kind of work is actually being done? Ah, I'll let the experts on the team worry about that. All I have to do is set up a schedule and then monitor that. The VP wants to know what's going on in this project? Ah, I'll let the architect talk to him.

None of this is "leadership". What you've done is let yourself become an impersonator. A weak, flaccid shell, someone who has no control over their project. Someone who doesn't inspire respect or confidence, from either the members of the team, or from management, or most important, from the client. Oh, you might be following the mechanical "process", but you aren't putting your stamp of competency on it. You're someone who no one else would have faith in to get the job done. Someone ultimately on the way out, and deservedly so.

Is that the kind of PM you want to be?

Sure, go for it. It makes more job opportunities for ME.

There was a time when I needed to hire a PM for my group. Though this might sound like I let my anality run wild, I went through over 40 interviews before I found the right person. The people I spoke with were all nice people, smart, and good team players. But they didn't have the kind of native leadership mentality that I was looking for. I wanted someone who had that special spark of interest in what the work was actually about. Someone who would dig into it, and learn about it well enough so that when he worked with the team, he fundamentally understood it to the level where he could drive the team to make the right decisions. The person needed to be assertive without being overbearing, knowledgeable without being arrogant, a net communicator instead of a pontificator, and someone who highly valued good teamwork and could seamlessly leverage it to produce the kinds of positive results I wanted.

That last point deserves some elaboration. You always hear about how important "team work" is, and how that leads to critical "consensus building". While that's true, it's also hogwash. As a leader, you don't want to build *consensus*. You want to meet or preferably exceed the objectives that you're being measured on. To do that, you have to drive your team to arrive at an agreement which supports those objectives. To succeed in doing that, you have to collaborate with your team so that they derive a sense of ownership for that agreement. But you have to be able to steer that collaboration to the outcome that you want. That means you better know what you want, but it also means that you can't just let the collaboration float along to some vague, indeterminate, or unanticipated result. You need to nail it down, and it has to agree with what you've wanted all along. It's called "engineering the consensus". (Or, it is now, since I just made that up.)

Or, to put it another way...

Major CS+PM Point: *Leadership is the ability to drive a group of people to a consensus agreement which supports your point of view.*

Think that sounds distasteful? Yeah, it's lonely at the top. You don't have to get all prickly about it, but if you like being on the top, and want to stay there, you better figure out how to define what you want and then know how to get it from your team.

But, what about collaboration? You put all these people on your team because they supposedly knew something about the work that needs to get done, right? Here's the slippery slope that you want to avoid.

People come in two parts: 1) the expertise they have for a given area, and 2) everything else. You select a person to interview for the "expertise" part, because who actually reads the parts of a resume about what they do in their spare time and all that other fluffy gorp? But when you interview someone for a job, you skip over the "expertise" part, and go right to wandering through the "everything else" part of that person. Explore all that touchy feely stuff. You know, to *connect* with them on a *personal level*. Establish a *bond* with them. Find out what how they'd *fit into your group*. See if they're a Yankees fan. (Just kidding!)[37]

It's important to find out what kind of personal context a person has which might affect your team. It can go either way, but typically, your first thought is to be scared stiff that the person might blow up your team into little, tiny pieces. Or worse, they may be so good that they're more qualified for your job than *you* are, and your boss might accidentally find that out, to your detriment.

---

[37] Not.

So, what you end up doing for most of the half-hour that you've calendared for the interview is to shoot the breeze. Why? Because it's fun. Relaxing. Or, because you made your mind up right away that the person just isn't going to cut it, so you have most of the half-hour to kill. But the point is that, for whatever set of reasons, you don't spend enough time focusing on the "expertise" part of the person. And you may end up liking the person so much that you hire him without really finding out if he has the actual skills you need. That can get really dicey because now you've made a friend that you may end up having to fire, which makes the person an ex-friend pretty quickly.

But, there's a flip side to this, too. You may get the perfunctory smalltalk[38] over with in a few seconds, because, what the heck, you don't really care about the person *as a person* anyway. People are just widgets, replaceable cogs, and your job is to focus on where to plug them in best, you won't have to actually marry the person. So, you run through the last 29 of your 30 minutes with him, testing him, asking him to write code[39], or create a marketing

---

[38] Sometimes, the talk is so superficial that it's not good enough to be called "smalltalk", so it's called "microtalk" instead. Most interviews are "picotalk".

[39] I went on an interview at a small tech company one time. Ahead of that, they sent me an architecture manual for the main computer they were developing. When I got to the interview, the first thing

slogan, or you challenge him with cutesy idiot questions to probe into his... whatevers. And, he lives up to your expectations, and you hire him, and find out pretty quickly that the guy is one of those slimy cringe-inducing types, and you end up firing him after 2 weeks. Not real productive.

The problem in all this, which is the slope you've been sliding down, is that in both cases, you've failed to realize that *people are a total package*. You can't just focus on one part or another of someone. When you're deciding to hire someone, you have to understand *all* of the parts of that person, because in the end, there aren't multiple parts. A person only has one part. And that is *the person*.

I was looking to hire a programmer into my group at one time. A candidate came through who was just out of school. He had some pretty good background as an intern, and seemed to know about computers pretty well. And he was impossible to not like. I

---

they asked me to do was to design a program to solve a particular problem, and to then code it in the assembler language for their system. After I barfed at that, and said, ha ha, funny people, I can't do that, they said "But we sent you our architecture manual ahead of time so you could study it. If you really wanted this job, you would have done that, to show us how much you wanted us to hire you." They said, come back in a week and we'll try this again. And I literally memorized the manual during that time, and came back, and wrote a beautiful program in their assembler code. And then took a job someplace else. I would never work for smarmy bastards like that.

mean, he was a terrific young man. Friendly, good sense of humor. The thing with him was that he was recovering from a significant illness, and that took up a lot of his time. You couldn't help but admire his gumption in dealing with that, which was substantial. Now, that's not the kind of thing you can talk about in an interview. But it made me focus more on the "everything else" side of him than on the "expertise" side. So, I glossed over his technical skills, because I really liked him as a person. And I ended up hiring him.

I know you expect me to say at this point that he didn't work out and I ended up having to fire him, and I went through years of shrink time because of that. But, no. It turns out that he was a great programmer for his level. He did a wonderful job. And everyone on my team, and in our organization, really liked him. So, things worked out. I was lucky. It could have worked out much differently, and I've seen that happen too often.

You've been taught in head-shaping school that everyone has their own unique and valuable perspectives and skills they can bring onto your team, which can make wondrous and valuable contributions toward getting the work done. But, oddly enough, it's true! The people you bring onto your team are supposedly adults, and really can provide useful insights which help the team get the work done. All you have to do is get them to actually *share* that with everyone else on the team.

How do you do that? Simple. *Collaborate* with them.

What's that mean?

Someone wouldn't be on your radar for recruiting to your team if they didn't have something on the ball. They are mature, self-actualized, well-trained people, who know what they're talking about. For the most part, anyway. Some more than others, maybe. You can sit down with each one of them, and talk about their individual parts of the project, and have a degree of success. Or, you can talk with them all, together, and you'll find out that there are more interdependencies than you realized, and that people like to help each other out with things. There's a synergy that happens when you get a team together, something more than just the team members taken individually, and as a leader, you need to foster that and make sure it grows. Why, because you want to charge them up for some work, turn them loose, and let them take care of themselves? Retired on the job, are you?

You don't get off that easy. No, collaboration takes work on your part. You need to get the team together on a regular basis. Agile tells you to do this at the end of every day, in your scrum meeting. That's great, but why limit it? It used to be the case where you could wander around the hallways and stop by the offices of all your people and chat them up a little. It was a great opportunity to check the water temperature of the team, and see who's hot about something and who's not. And, you can toss in a question or two about how the *work* is going, and ask what issues you can help out with, and generally spy on your folks. NO NO, that's not what I meant.[40] I meant, it's a great way to interact with your team. This wandering around had an actual name, MBWA, or Management By Walking Around. I loved it, because, for me, it was a natural fit, since I liked to avoid work whenever possible. But, really, this was a very important part of staying plugged into what your team was up to.

Of course, in today's world, MBWA isn't always possible, because who has offices anymore? Work space is all huge cube farms now, thanks to some lame office efficiency expert from medieval times who thought taking the office walls down would facilitate better communications. Sure it does. Now you have to listen to everyone else on the phone, or clicking away at their keyboards, or just pissing and moaning to themselves about something. And then you get the ones who like to hang over the cube wall

---

[40] Oh, come on. Sure it is.

and ask you questions about nonsense stuff, interrupting your nap time.

But even cube farms are going the way of the dodo. The internet has provided a terrific way to outsource work to employees who are located in every little Podunk nook and cranny around the country, or really, the entire world. No one is co-located these days. Everyone lives at the end of your phone. You never meet your teammates personally. You never even see them. Mostly, you just yak at them in conference calls, and shoot emails back and forth. It's a totally sterile, impersonal environment now.

However, there's hope. A tool was invented way back in the days of character-based terminals to let people "chat" with each other. It allowed you to talk with your teammates by typing what you wanted to say into the tool, which would display that on the other person's screen, and they would respond back to you, pretty much in real time. "Chatting" has evolved (if you can call it that) into more contemporary tools, like AOL Instant Messenger (or what it used to do, anyway), Apple's iMessage, Lotus Sametime, GoogleTalk, Windows Messenger, and lots of other messaging tools. Now, people have so much more to do in meetings than actually having to listen to what's going on. Messaging is an office social phenomenon.

And what it lets you, as a PM, do is to do your MBWA electronically. Now, you can ping anyone on your team, any time you want to, without having to actually get your *derriere maximus* out of your chair. Or, less caustically, you can chat with people wherever they are, because you probably work at home now, and your team is spread across 5 or 6 states and 3 other countries.

What I'm saying here is that a very important leadership skill is *relationship management*. Get to know your teammates. Find out what interests them and what they can't stand. These are people, you know, and it's free to be nice to them. This doesn't mean to get into the gossip weeds with them, but if you treat them openly and honestly, and view them as professionals and not interchangeable cogs in the great corporate wheel, they'll respond to you. Of course, you'll develop closer bonds with some people more than others. But the minute you've been unfair or nasty to someone, you've lost them, and it's incredibly difficult to fix that. You need people to feel good about the work, and about you, and about each other.

There are those who would disagree with this. Some management types think a stick to beat people with is a better leverage point than being respectful toward them. You get people to do better work by instilling fear in them. Make them uncomfortable in their position, and they'll get their act in gear. Train them to think that they could lose their job at any instant if they don't produce, and they'll produce.

There's a word that describes this mentality, and it's this: crap.

People who act like that toward others are falling prey to their own overwhelming inferiority complex. In their heart of hearts, they're so unsure about themselves that they feel the only way they can get people to do what's needed is to dictate to them, in no uncertain terms. There's no sense of collaboration with them. Everything is one-way: THEIR way. They know best. The people on their team are stupid, terrifying creatures, and they need to be whipped into line. They think of themselves as the lion tamer who has a particularly unruly animal to control. Might makes right.

Well, that approach does work for a while, at least until the peasants stage the inevitable uprising.

But you get more ants with sugar than vinegar.

Here's the point in all this...

Major CS+PM Point: *Treat people with respect and view them as the professionals that they are, and they will go the extra mile for you.*

No one likes to be treated like roadkill, even if that's what companies want to turn most of their employees into these days. Sometimes there's a real urgency to get a piece of work done, and things can get very net and often abrupt, and you don't have time to chit chat or share the normal niceties that you like. But those times are rare. And even when those times happen, there's no need to be rude or aggressive toward your team. You're all in the same boat, and there's no use in you drilling holes in the bottom of it, because you'll all sink together if you do that. If you're in a crunch and you need your team to step up for some heroic work, they'll be more apt to go along with that if they respect you and share your sense of urgency and ownership about things. And that only comes through treating them as professionals and collaborating with them. And having your team respect you doesn't happen overnight, either. It takes a substantial amount of time and prep work on your part to demonstrate enough to them so that they respect you. And you have to maintain that over time. It's called "earning it". Respect isn't given to you, and you aren't entitled to it. But respect is a fleeting thing. If you treat your team like semi-trained monkeys, they'll pee on your shoes before telling you to buzz off. Bye, bye respect. And THAT, you would have earned.

Socialism

Major CS+PM Point: *If you want to be an effective project manager, you need to be a good socialist first.*

Whoa. Leading off a new chapter with a Major Point? Nothing like jumping right into things.

Now, this isn't a book about politics. Oh, sure, there are certainly politics at work inside any business organization, because there are *people* inside those organizations. Where there are people, there are politics. That is, of course, a main focus for this book -- how to weave your way through all the organizational politics that you face as a project manager. But, there are politics, and then there are *politics*, like the kind that happens in governments. National politics. Global politics. All that happy stuff you read about in the papers (or, more accurately, on the web sites for all the papers that don't actually have print editions any more because of, well... the internet and all those web sites...). There are things you don't talk about at work. Religion is the biggie. And in a similar vein, *those* kinds of politics are another, since they're actually a kind of religious belief system all by themselves. Just. Don't. Go. There.

But since you live and breath the other kinds of politics (the work related ones) those are fair game for dissection. There's a fine line (maybe not so fine) between politics and gossip, though, and crossing that boundary puts you in soap opera land, which is verboten for the non-catty among us.

For those of us who *are* catty, though, which is pretty much all of us, what we're really talking about here is something called "social socialism".

No, this isn't a self-redundant term. If we consider the *socialism* part, we know that this means "sharing the wealth". It also means "sharing the responsibility", which is a hidden feature of socialism. If we all want to be *equals*, which is a basic tenet of socialism, we can't expect someone else to do the decision making so we can just sit back and get all passive about things. Oh, no. We need to be a part of the decision making process. Why? Because *everyone* is part of the decision making process. Not that everyone is exactly *equal* in this, of course. Some people are more equal than others, as

Orwell would say. Like, for instance, the project manager, who is the most equal among equals[41]. That is actually a more egalitarian statement than you might realize, as we will soon discover.

Now, looking at social socialism, you have to ask yourself what "wealth" there is on a project to share. What you might normally think of when imagining a "project" is slipping schedules, depleted budgets, excessive resource contention, and scope creep that would sink the Titanic. But there are nuggets buried in these tales of woe that are, believe it or not, positive. Suppose, for instance, that someone on your project has had a breakthrough[42], and has figured out a way to get a task done *ahead of schedule*. I know, that sounds unimaginable, but part of project management folklore is that things like that have, in fact, actually happened on certain mythical projects.

As it turns out in our little imaginary scenario, that breakthrough has had a ripple effect on all the tasks in the schedule which follow it, and they are all completed ~~not as far behind schedule as they would have been~~ ahead of schedule, too. This is goodness, and everyone on the team feels peachy about it. So, as the project manager, how should you react?

---

[41] I don't always drink Kool Aid. But when I do, I prefer DOS Techies.

[42] As opposed to the standard *breakdown*. See also "Work Breakdown Structure". Oooo... a little PM humor there.

This is where *share the wealth* comes in.

Of course, you *recognize* the person who had the breakthrough. Keep it proportional to the actual significance of the breakthrough, certainly. But don't just take the opportunity to tell the person that they did a great job. You have to *make* the opportunity to do that. Go back to the chapter on Leadership, when the point was made about *treating your team like the professionals they are*. Now's a good time to do that.

It's amazing how much simple recognition can do for team morale. I heard Paul O'Neill of the New York Yankees tell a story about this. When a player had a good game, he was interviewed on the radio afterwards, and he was given a free meal at a local restaurant as an award. This was good advertising for the restaurant, of course. And these guys were making millions, so the cost of a nice meal was just noise to them. But the players still fought like crazy to get interviewed so that they could get that free meal. Why? It certainly wasn't the money. As it turns out, the important thing to them was getting recognized publicly for having a great game. They could strut around the clubhouse and wave the free meal ticket in the air and tell everyone that they had a better game than anyone else on the team. Sure, it sounds (more than) a little immature to do, but these are pro athletes, after all, so that comes with the territory.

There is a scale of perspective here, too, though. In 1990, Rickey Henderson had just signed a new contract with the Oakland A's, and said during an interview that he was disappointed with it. Oh, it wasn't the money, he said. That was all just fine, especially since it set a record for the time. But he had expected a bonus in the contract for when he surpassed Lou Brock in stealing bases, too, and he hadn't gotten that. The bonus just happened to be a brand new Ferrari Testarossa. Nice wheels. But he said he was disappointed that he didn't get the bonus because "the little things mean more than the big things to me[43]". A new Ferrari, a "little thing"... Thanks for the insight, Rickey. Of course, consider the source... a few years before that, he decided to not cash his $1 million bonus check. He framed it and hung it on his wall instead. Hey, Rickey! Take a picture of the check and hang *that* on the wall. But CASH THE CHECK.

Obviously, unless you happen to be Warren Buffett and you're on "Undercover Boss" at the time, playing at being a project manager, you most likely won't be thinking of giving your teammate a new Ferrari because she finished a task ahead of time. That might be a nice thing to do, but you may want to

---

[43] See http://articles.philly.com/1990-03-30/sports/25901896_1_stolen-base-record-rangers-general-manager-oakland-outfielder-rickey-henderson .

consider the precedent it could set for good things that happen in the future. What you would more likely do is to say "Thanks" to the person, or something witty like "Good work". Don't go overboard and get too effusive about it. That makes people really uncomfortable, and will work against morale instead of for it. Keep things in perspective. And don't wear it out, either, by recognizing every single little thing that your team does. Leave the gold stars at home.

You may notice that in doing recognition like this, you're being this thing called *nice*. That gets to the "social" part of social socialism. A big part of this is that not only is it nice to be nice, but being nice is free. As in, *free*. That doesn't mean it's easy. Not everyone is a natural at being nice, and they have to work at it. Some people live their entire lives with their hair on fire. Not nice. Others are *so* nice, they can't drive their teams to get anything done, because they're wearing their arms out by patting everyone on the back all the time. That might be nice, but it won't get you anywhere. You have to find a middle ground where you can be nice, and also be effective in driving your team to meet your objectives. This is part of the craftsmanship of being a project manager. There are no formulas for it. You get this skill mostly because you have the genes for it, and also because you emulate others you've worked with who have the gift. You learn by observing successful people.

Also, notice what you *aren't* doing. When someone on your team does something well, you give them credit for that. You don't keep the glory for yourself. You spread it around. That keeps the people happy. Think of it this way... *you don't own credit for work other people do*. You are only the guardian for that credit. Your team gives you repositories of credit that you can draw from when it's time to dispense a little to someone on your team. But you can't keep it. You can't bathe in it. You can't hold onto it. It is yours only to give away.

And when you do that, and do it right, you not only create a happy team, but you create something else:

Respect.

And you create its cousin, *Trust*, too.

Some things are worth repeating.

Respect and trust are two-way streets. Your team will only respect you when you respect them. And, they will only trust you when you trust them. It sounds so... grown up.

But the funny thing about this is that when you give other people credit for doing good work, *you look good, too*. Happiness is contagious, viral even. Happy employees can even make management ~~suspicious~~ happy.

So, the point is this:

Major CS+PM Point: *It is in your own self-interest to treat your team with respect by appropriately recognizing a job well done.*

But just recognizing someone for doing a good job isn't all that's entailed in social socialism. The other part is involving them in the decision making process.

Hey, you're the boss, right? Why the heck would you want to give some of your authority away by letting someone on your team make decisions? Isn't that your job?

Well, the simple answer to that is: No. And the reason for that is this: *because you don't know everything*. That's right, there are others on your team who actually know more than you do. That might be in a narrow area, or it might be larger in scope. But remember back to what was discussed in the chapter on Domain Expertise, that the reason why you have these people on your team is because *they know things that you do not*. And be thankful for that, because your brain isn't big enough to hold all those teensy little bits of information that your team as a whole has in their heads.

Here's the point: the people on your team are pros. That's why they're there. They really, honestly, do absolutely know what they're talking about. And they sure as shooting know more about their area of expertise than you do. In fact, your team is probably made up of godlike creatures called SMEs, or Subject Matter Experts. Why are they called that? Because they are *experts* in their *subject* area. Duh.

And that means they can do a lot more than just pontificate about things. They can *do* things. And they know what things need to be done.

Your job is not to do what they are there to do. Your job is to *leverage their expertise*. Your team has spent their entire professional lives learning precisely what they were brought onto your team to do. Your job is to channel that expertise into results which meet your objectives.

As Casey Stengel said: Managing is getting paid for home runs someone else hits.

How can you channel all that great expertise into the results you need?

You've already shared the wealth. Now it's time to *share the responsibility*, too.

Let's suppose that your project has been going along just fine, with people getting their tasks done on time, and you never run out of funding, and everyone is just happy happy happy. Then, along comes reality, and bounces a huge wrench into the middle of your glass menagerie of fun, and all the little animals inside start to break. Oh, what to do?

Your first reaction, after running to the fridge for some comfort food, is to *call a meeting* with your team. Why? Well, to find out where the finger of blame should point, of course. NO, that's not right[44]. The first thing you need to do is to triage the problem to find out how serious it is so you can determine the spread of impact to your project. Who knows better what the breakage to your plan is than the people who broke it?

So, you get everyone together and run through the situation. Once you've figured out how serious things are, you get all transparent about things and ask them, "OK, I'm looking for suggestions here. What do we do now?" Great leadership there.

Actually, it *is* great leadership. You could have chosen to illuminate your team with the grace of your superior wisdom instead and just tell them what was going to happen. And then you'd proceed to outline every single step they'd take, and you'd let them know how you'd keep track of everything, because you have to make sure they didn't screw things up again. Like that.

But, you want to succeed as a project manager. And dictating things to your team is a sure way to *not*

---

[44] Oh, maybe it's not *right*, exactly, but you'll do it anyway, just to find out what trump cards there are to keep in your back pocket to use later on. You know, in the career post mortem. Wait... I mean, in the exec review.

succeed. These folks are the experts, remember, not you. So, you not only depend on them to know what has to get done, you rely on them to share that with the rest of the team, too. You let them brainstorm about all the various possible things that could be done, and you get them to rule things out that won't work, and build on things that will. And you facilitate this discussion until things start to gel, and an action plan starts to develop. It's like telling the future with your Magic 8 Ball. You ask it a question, and the answer slowly starts to reveal itself. This is what we call the Magical Kingdom of Teamwork.

Remember back to the chapter on Leadership, though. Your job as the leader of this Merry Band of Cognoscenti is to get them to agree on a plan that satisfies not just the goals and objectives of the team, but supports the things that you're measured on, too. Normally, you'd hope those would be one and the same. Sometimes they actually are. But the point is that you probably already have a good sense for what the right course of action needs to be. So, what you need to do with the team is to refine that into a recovery plan that everyone agrees on. And, of course, agrees with your opinion about what needs to happen. But what you've done in the process is to conscript the team over to your opinion about things. And made them happy to be part of that process, to boot.

And, *you've shared the responsibility for the plan.* That is great socialism. And the point is this:

Major CS+PM Point: *Risks are as much a part of project planning as accomplishments, so it's key to spread them around, too.*

But, why is that so important? Sure, it's goodness to groom your team and keep them happy and productive. And it's always nice to share things with each other. But why go to all this work to get their opinions about things and fracture your authority as the Project Manager among them?

Because, some problems can't be fixed within your team. You need help from above. No, not Divine Intervention. Management Intervention[45].

There are many problems you can fix within your own team. All those little irritants that pop up every so often are mostly just part of the daily churn of activities that we all enjoy. And no one above you really wants to hear about that. It's just part of the job to fix them.

But, sometimes there are problems that are larger in scope, and to fix them will cost more than you can afford, and will require lots of warm bodies to

---

[45] Which management thinks are one and the same.

handle, too. And that is something you can't do alone.

You know what they say are the three most important things when it comes to selling real estate? Right... "location, location, and location." Well, when it comes to project management, the three most important things when you're trying to keep your project ship from sinking are "escalate, escalate, and escalate." The point is that if you can't fix a problem immediately, do NOT hide it. Learn how to escalate, at the appropriate time, to the appropriate management, with the appropriate bells and whistles ringing.

But why do that?

Because you've already shared the responsibility for recovering from a problem. Now you need to *share the accountability* for it, too.

All good socialism.

Consider the alternative. Suppose your plan is well and truly broken. And further consider that you've chosen to keep all this to yourself, and you haven't told management about it. You've let it fester and grow and get to the point where it's bursting through its seams. It has become an overwhelming monster, and you can't avoid telling management about it any longer. So, you slither into the Project Management Council and keep your face glued to the floor and say in your meekest little voice, "My project is broken and I can't fix it."

Oh, the horror.

You obviously want to avoid these kinds of career limiting situations. But, how?

The most effective way to do that is to recognize early on that your team has a serious problem, and then do the groundwork to prepare your management about it. Don't cry wolf, but don't delay in letting them know that there's an issue percolating with the plan. Keep management aware of the steps you're taking to mitigate the problem. And, if it gets to the point where the plan is too broken to fix within your team, you can go to management and ask for their help, and you won't surprise them about it. The thing you need to realize is that *every time you talk with management, you're asking for their help, even if you don't think you are.* Why? Because these aren't write-only people. You can't just pour a problem onto them and not expect them to react. They will soak it up, and will illuminate *you* with their wisdom about how you should proceed. How many ways can you spell "discomfort"?

You can't always anticipate problems. Sometimes, they just happen, and you get to bask in their glory. But what you *can* do is to *get out in front of problems*. Control the situation before it controls you.

You can't do that if you don't tell people about what you're doing. In the world of project management, you need to make other people aware of what's going wrong with your project, and to demonstrate to them how you're fixing issues, and to enlist their help in resolving things when needed. With management, you're going to get their help whether you want it or not, so you might as well ask for it *on your own terms* so that you can control it. It's called "managing your management". You won't always succeed in doing that because, remember, it's a qualification for management to have your hair on fire 100 percent of the time. But it's a guarantee that you *will* have a short lifespan as a project manager if you don't socialize accountability for resolving problems.

What that ultimately means is this...

Major CS+PM Point: *Socializing accountability for resolving problems will go a long way toward making your life as a project manager more enjoyable. And longer.*

Faith

I'd like to expand on a point I made in the chapter about *Domain Expertise*, which was that no one knows everything about anything. Now, you might think that was just another cheap shot at managers[46]. But no, I was talking about how everyone knows a lot about something, and that's different than what someone else knows a lot about, so get the two of them together and you more than double your knowledge base. And, when you build a whole team of people like this, you have a lot more knowledge on your team than just the sum of the parts might indicate. Magic does happen.

---

[46] Which would have been incorrect, because if I had been talking about managers, I would have said something insightful about people who know nothing about anything. HAHA, kidding. Right?

But you, as the project manager, not only don't know all that everyone on your team does, you most likely don't know enough about what some particular person on your team knows to judge whether or not he's blowing smoke at you about something. But, you put that person on your team because he knows something about *something* which is important to the work you're doing. And, you trust him to be right about those things.

That is called "faith", where you *trust the unknown*. Faith is all around us. Normally, we're referring to religion when we talk about faith, but here, I'm just talking about this:

Major CS+PM point: *Faith is trusting that the people on your team really do know what they're talking about, and even if they stumble on things once in a while, that they'll keep at it until they get it right.*

Let me give an example of what faith can mean and show how common it really is.

Suppose you're putting in some extra hours over the weekend, and you're working at home. It's getting late in the day, and you start getting your sugar crash from all the sweetened coffee you've been drinking to keep from nodding off. In this dazed state, you figure that the best thing to revive you is *more sugar*, so you run to the kitchen and begin grazing through the cabinets to see what's hidden in there. And, lo and behold, you find a package of those super tasty bakery-made chocolate chip cookies that you got a few months ago and had totally forgotten about. And you think, *whoa, that's better right now than finding a pirate ship full of gold coins*. And you proceed to rip the package open, and you mangle a couple of cookies in your haste to get at them, and crumbs go flying all over the kitchen. And you realize, wait, I need something to help wash these things down my gullet. I need *milk*. And you run to the fridge, and see that it's just *empty* because this isn't the first time today that you've been grazing for eats, and the one thing that's really, absolutely gone is *milk*. AH, you scream, you can't eat cookies without milk.

So, you run to your car and jump in, because lacking a personal cow, you have to go to the store to buy more milk. But, then you jump out of the car and run back in the house because you discover that you forgot to take your car keys with you. And you spend an entire half hour looking for the stupid keys because *someone* put them in some ridiculous place like under a couch cushion or behind a radiator or inside the ceiling or someplace other than on the galdang little hook on the wall by the door out to the garage where they're supposed to be. And you run to the hook and *there* are your car keys, and you can't figure out who would actually put them *there*. And you run back outside and jump in your car again, and put your key in the ignition and turn it and the engine starts up and you grab hold of this big metal rod thing sticking out of the floor and pull back on it and these little lights on your dashboard change from "P" to "D" and your car suddenly lurches forward and smashes into the new lawn tractor you just bought and your front bumper falls off and your airbag explodes out of the steering wheel and you're in a world of hurt. Like that.

OK, let's review: yes, your car was facing into the garage, and you should have put the transmission into *reverse* to back out of the garage instead of into *drive*.

But, aside from that little learning experience, here's a question: when you put the key in the ignition and turned it, did you know what happened to the car as a result of doing that? I mean, you turn the key, and the engine starts, but do you know what the sequence of events was to make that actually work? Unless you happen to be the automotive engineer who designed the car's ignition circuitry, you don't. But it works. And it works every time you turn the key in the ignition. And because it works all the time, you figure it's going to keep on working the next time you try it. And that means you have *faith* that it will work, because you have no clue about how it *actually* works, but your experience has taught you that it *will* work. And it does, right up until the time your car's battery dies. Then, it won't.

Let me make this a little more granular.

When you turned the key and the engine started, nothing really spectacular happened to the car. Apart from your lack of attention to how to drive it, the car didn't fall apart, and the engine didn't come flying through the hood. Why not?

Let's just look at why the engine didn't come flying through the hood.

It turns out that there's little thing called an "engine bolt" that holds the engine in place. Actually, there are a number of these bolts, and they all work together to hold the engine in place. But, let's focus on just one of them right now.

This engine bolt is really just a short metal rod, with a flat head on one end and threads on the other. There's a bracket on the engine block which has threads that match the ones on the bolt, and another bracket in the engine compartment that is attached to the chassis of the car. So, you slide the bolt through the chassis bracket, and you screw it into the bracket on the engine, and the bolt holds the engine in place. Ta da! That means that the engine doesn't shake and bounce around enough to go flying through the hood when you turn it on, and you can avoid the problem of the engine launching out of the car and going flying through the air across the street and through the new bay window your neighbor just had installed and setting their house on fire and then their lawyer calling you and talking all this indecipherable legal mumbo jumbo to you and all that. Nice.

But the point is that this engine bolt isn't just a regular bolt. No, no, life isn't that simple. See, it has to be designed to a set of specific criteria that keeps the bolt from breaking apart when the engine starts. You know, to keep the engine from flying through the hood. For instance, the metal that the bolt is made out of needs to be strong enough to resist the kinds of forces that the bolt will experience when the engine is turned on. When you start the engine, it would naturally begin to shake and rattle and twist around, and that will stress the bolt in all kinds of directions. The engine will try to move the bolt back and forth, and will pull on it to stretch it, and will bang it around in circles, and will do all these awful things to it. Naughty engine. And the bolt can't fail when that happens, so it has to be made out of a material that resists those kinds of forces. And the engine will get HOT, so the bolt material can't get soft or brittle or expand too much when it gets heated. Then, the threads on the end of the bolt need to match the threads on the engine block bracket pretty precisely, because if they don't, then the bolt will get loose and may unscrew itself which will let the engine fly through the hood, which is never good policy. And the bolt has to be manufactured at a really low cost, since you can't have bolts like this costing a thousand bucks because you use a bazillion of these things and that will make your car price skyrocket. And you better make sure you make enough of these bolts because the car manufacturers use them by the boatload, and if you run out, your business is toast. And you also need to make sure that you have enough trucks to ship these bolts out to the car companies, and that they run on time and *they* don't have defective engine bolts that will let *their* engines fly through their hoods, because the delivery trucks need to keep running on schedule.

Our simple little engine bolt turns out to have lots and lots of moving parts to make it a successful product.

But, there's more.

At every step of the bolt's life, there are these things involved called "people". You may have read that these *people* things are frail and prone to accidents and mistakes, and that would be correct. In fact, if you line a bunch of them up, and whisper something into the ear of one of them, and then have that person whisper the same thing into the ear of the person next to them, and so on and so forth until the last person there has been whispered to, you'll find that the last person heard something entirely different from what the first person actually said. Why? Because these people are what we call "human", and we know beyond doubt that humans are undependable, erratic creatures.

So, the successful bolt depends on finding a way to minimize the human tendency to be less than perfectly reliable. And the way the bolt solved this problem was to add more people to each step in its lifecycle.

This might seem counterintuitive, but we *are* talking about an engine bolt here, and I have yet to meet one of them with any credible education.

So... the point is that for every step of the bolt's development and manufacturing and distribution processes, there are multiple people involved. How many would that be?

Look at the effort that has to go into the development of the material used in the bolt. Someone has to know the basic formula for making the metal for the bolt. As it turns out, there is no such substance actually comprised of "metal". The thing we call "metal" is actually made from many things, like iron, and magnesium, and carbon, and silicon, and tungsten, and... hey, wake up! And there are different proportions of these substances that yield different characteristics. And the cost of different formulations of these things will affect the cost of the metal that the bolt is made of. And those proportions are determined by lots of testing and evaluation and research. And after a lot of trial and error, we finally get a type of "metal" that meets all the criteria for an engine bolt that we discussed before. Cool.

So, let's figure that ten people had to work together on the research for this metal. Then another ten people had to work on the testing of the metal to make sure it worked the way it needed to. And of course, those testers would have to go back to the researchers to get all the problems that they discovered in the metal fixed. Lots of discussions going on there. Now suppose that, once the metal formula was decided on, then the designers had to actually design the bolt. They'd have to take into account the properties of the metal, and would design threads, for example, that weren't too thick, which would make them too bulky to screw into a bracket, or too thin, which would make them bend too much and eventually flatten out to the point of failure. Suppose it takes five people to work together on the thread design. Now, that's not quite accurate, because these people have to work with the team doing the thread design for the engine block bracket, to make sure all these threads will actually fit together. But let's ignore the engine bracket folks for now. (Sorry, guys.)

Once the designers are done, then the bolt has to be tested. Suppose there are five people involved in that. But, when they're done, and the bolt meets all the criteria it's supposed to, we have a finished product, and it only took thirty people to produce it.

But, wait... now we have to manufacture the bolt. Oh, gosh, there's a whole supply chain at work here. We have to find all the right materials that make up the metal according to what the researchers said, and get them all put together, which means mixing them together and melting them into a soup not unlike what you had at your mother-in-law's last week[47]. Then we have to make the molds that we pour the molten metal into to form the bolts. And we have to have the machines that can polish the bolts so all the little extra pieces of metal that come from the manufacturing process can be scoured away. And we have to have the boxes that we put the bolts into so we can ship them out. And the common thread through all this is *people*, and there are scads of them. Why? Well, because once you move from researching a product to building it, the scale of things that have to happen increases dramatically, and that takes a lot more people. But, all these people

[47] Man, am I kidding about THAT. I can just see an activist group of mothers-in-law protesting outside my house over that one. Kidding, Moms! And my mother-in-law was a TERRIFIC cook, and made really delicious soup.

make a LOT of engine bolts, and we're only worrying about just one right now, so let's decide on how many people are actually involved in manufacturing just the one bolt. Say it's another ten.

Then we have to ship the boxes of bolts out to the car manufacturers, and that takes more people. Let's just say we need someone to take the boxes of bolts and move them to the trucks that will deliver them, and then someone to drive the trucks, and someone to supply the coffee that the drivers need when they drive all night, and someone... well, it can go on forever. Let's just say that for our one little bolt, it might take five more people to get it from the plant to the customer, and another five there to receive it and get it to the assembly line, and actually use it.

All in all, we're up to about fifty people involved in the research, development, manufacture, distribution, and use of that one tiny little bolt. Now, go back to the example of the whisper game, and see how difficult it is to get fifty people to communicate with each other consistently and accurately. Here's a hint: it's pretty hard. But, evidently, it happens, because we haven't read about very many engines flying through hoods lately.

Now consider that cars are made from a few more parts than just our little engine bolt. Cars typically have around 3,500 different parts. That's a lot of parts. So, if it takes fifty people just to make one silly little engine bolt, there are 3,499 more parts in a car that we have to worry about. And, gosh, that's like, what... 175,000 people who have to work together to build the car you just started so you could get to the store and buy milk to go along with your cookies.

And the amazing thing isn't that the car works so well for as long as it does. The mind-bending thing is that the car works *at all*.

With that many people having to collaborate, the number of interaction points is exponential. The probability of incorrect communications is so high that it's essentially meaningless to calculate. Yet, when you turn your key, the engine starts, and it will keep on starting for a very long time. We think we know how this all happens. There is a very large scale psychology at work in this, and also a history of analyzing quality in organizations to minimize errors. But the point is that when we turn the key in the ignition, *we* as individual users don't really know how it all works. It just does. And we depend on that. We have *faith* that it will work. And that faith is rewarded every day.

As a project manager, you will most likely not know everything about what's going on in your project. You may, for instance, need to get a batch of servers built, and the folks who do that will know every little tiny step in the process of getting that done. But when you put your project plan together, you'd use more storage than any computer could ever hold if you tried putting every single step of that into your plan. But, on the other hand, you need to put at least a *little* detail in your plan about the work involved, because there's *work* involved, and that means that people's time is involved, and that means there are labor costs involved. So, there's a certain amount of project management craftsmanship needed here to make sure your plan is sufficiently detailed to adequately describe the work to the point where your team knows who has to do what, but not overloaded with minutia that takes all your time to include, and then track, and all your team's time just specifying. There's a middle ground that you need to find. And that takes collaboration and experience.

The point in this is that the people you have on your team really do know what they're doing. If they didn't, they wouldn't be on your team. Ostensibly, anyway. So, you need to trust that they will deliver what's needed. Sure, sometimes things break down, so you do need to monitor and control things, especially so you can report back to management about the state of affairs in your project. But you need to have a lot of faith that the people on your team will be professional enough to get their work done, and to let you know when they can't for whatever reasons[48]. This comes back to leadership, and how that depends on the trust of your team in *you*. You see, faith is a two-way street. You have to earn the trust of your team, just like they have to earn your trust, and all that results in being able to have enough faith in each other that you can work together, and be productive, and all that happy gorp. Don't micromanage your team. That is death for the kind of trust and faith you need to pull a project off successfully time and again. Put the right team in place, work with them so that everyone understands what is involved, provide the support and resources they need, and let them get things done. Have faith in them, and they will return the favor.

---

[48] Except if they happen to win the lottery, in which case you've already seen them for the last time ever. And, forget about getting a Christmas card from them.

ManageMental

I make a lot of comments in this book which otherwise erudite people might consider to be attempts at pissing management right the heck off. Not true. OK, not *entirely* true, depending on how you define "entirely". All I'm trying to do is get this point across:

Major CS+PM point: *There are different universes of thought to deal with when managing projects.*

Not all of these universes are governed by the same rules. You'd think that, hey, we're all in the same *room* here, talking about the same *thing*, so why are these managers so disconnected from reality? What you fail to realize is that they are not disconnected from reality at all. They are quite well connected to *their* reality, but just happen to be disconnected from *yours*. And they may be thinking the same thing about you.

Of course, their reality and your reality are probably not all that far apart, but they are likely distinguished from each other by some key elements. For instance, you might think that getting your buddy Joe to work on your project is of such importance that the world will stop revolving on its axis if that doesn't happen. But, Joe's Manager (note the capital letter) thinks that there might be some other frivolous project where Joe's time would be better spent. And, a discussion would ensue about the merits of your project versus that other useless thing the PM over there has the nerve to call a "project", and you'll wonder what planet Joe's Manager comes from.

And "planets" bring us to "science".

The discussion in vogue these days in the world of science is about The Big Bang Theory. No, I don't mean the cringefest sitcom on cable by that name[49]. I mean how our universe happened. We have this amazing theory that purports to define all the wonderful rules and laws that our universe works under, and how these things conspire to make it into what we know and love today. But, the even newer

---

[49] Actually, parts of the show are pretty funny. Not enough to make the whole show worth watching, but it sometimes has its moments.

science gab is how there are actually *multiple* universes out there, and each one has its *own* set of rules and laws that are somewhat different than the other universes. No one really knows for sure. It would appear that on the way to defining quantum physics, some gaps showed up in the equations, and they had to be filled in. Hence, dark matter and multiple universes. This is what I love about science. If there's a gap in a theory, then someone makes stuff up to fill it in. If you want to extend a theory, well, just tack some pudding onto the side of it, and you have a brand new theory.

This is what the management universe is like. There are rules that it abides by. These rules are similar to the rules that apply in your universe, but are different enough to make them utterly disorienting to the uninitiated. And, since you don't understand them, you never know which rules are made out of pudding and which rules are made from something more substantive.

To understand this, let's start from a basis of commonality. Given how many rules and laws there are in a universe, it's statistically improbable that when going from one universe to another, there would be a complete lack of overlap between the sets of rules for each of them. There would have to be some small set of laws that would be the same. But, what that overlap would be is not quite apparent. You need to have the appropriate visual filter engaged to see these things. That is where your PM Goggles come into play. Just look at the cover of this book to see what these goggles look like. You may notice a slight rose-colored tint to their lenses, which is required to provide the appropriate skew to your perception of reality. Just put them on, and you now have all the tools you need to understand how management sees things.

Imagine that you're back in the conference room, still having that infernal debate with Joe's Manager about conscripting poor Joe onto your team. But, now you have your PM Goggles on, which shifts reality just a bit toward management's perspective. Stand up and move around the conference room. What do you see?

Perhaps the first thing you'd notice is that the people sitting around the table are not all quite the same. Most of the people have a large scarlet letter "T" emblazoned on their foreheads. These people are the mythical creatures from the land of TechnoDungeon, to which they have been banished for perpetrating imperceptible slights and indignities upon the Great and Powerful Business. Notice how busy their hands are, their fingers flying over the screens of electronic apparatuses attached to the ends of their arms. The scowls on their faces provide a window into the tortured existence upon which they thrive. They mumble amongst themselves, their language an indecipherable stream of clicks and yips and punctuation marks.

Now, see the others sitting there at the table. They sip magic potions from mugs with stars and long-haired angels on them, the giant M clear for all to see. There is a glow about them, emanating in ripples of effervescent sheens to give luster to all around. Swirling about their heads in spirals of pastels and sparkles is the special air they breathe, the source of their limitless cognitive brilliance, which they will disburse to the fortunate few in minuscule portions. You are warmed by the sheer radiance of their presence, and are honored by the audience with them which they have seen fit to grant to a low and disdained speck of dust such as yourself.

Now, take your goggles off, and what do you see? Well, there's Joe's Manager, sitting there, messaging on his smartphone with someone else, ignoring you, slugging his Starbucks, along with all the other managers and technical people in your organization, also messaging with someone else, and likewise also ignoring you. Just a normal day at the quarry, moving slices of stone around the pit.

But you have the advantage now. You have glimpsed the Universe of Management, and have seen with your very own goggles what the true perception of the world is like for those so blessed to be entitled "manager". Yes, you have been truly tainted now, forever unable to see things any other way, a curse you will carry with you for the remainder of your mortal days...

OK, so you might think this is more than a little stretch here. Perhaps it is. But... perhaps it isn't. Let's decompose this to separate the wheat from the chaff.

You, as a PM, are mandated by the conditions of your PMP certification to wear blinders. After all, that is one of the values of "projects", which is the discipline required to maintain your focus on only that one project. That is also one of the rules in your universe. You can't worry about all the other things going on around you, unless you happen to have multitudinous projects under your wing. But let's not think about that horror right now.

You need to focus on one team, and one scope of work, and one budget, and one plan[50]. You can't spend your precious time worrying about what your buddy Joe is doing. That's his problem. Oh, you go to lunch with him, and he whines to you about all the problems he's having on his project, and you respond by whining right back about your project problems. But then you each go back to your very own Ivory Tower project cloister and say to yourselves, *man,*

---

[50] That makes 4 things you have to worry about as a PM. Too hard. I went into programming because you only had to learn how to count up to 1. You know... 0,1,0,1,0,0,1,1. Like that. Simple.

*am I glad I don't have to worry about HIS stuff, with
all the junk I have to wrestle with on my own project.*
Spinning plates come to mind.

One project, one view, one set of rules in your
solitary little universe.

That is, of course, until you discover that you
have a dependency on what Joe's doing. Ack[51]. Then
you have to go talk with him, and let him know that
you need something from him so you can finish your
project work. See, it turns out that your two projects
aren't as independent of each other as you had
originally thought. *That* is a major game changer.
Now you have to blend some rules from your
universe with some of Joe's rules.

For instance, now you have to put a task in your
project plan like "Tell Joe what you need from him
and when", and another one like "Test this stuff out
with Joe" and another one like "Go talk with Joe's
Manager because he's not getting my stuff done on
schedule" and so on. All these little touch points have
to be added to *your* plan, and then linked with things
in *Joe's* plan, so that you can get your one little
measly tidbit of function done by him, when you
need it. And your life had been so simple before all
this.

---

[51] Think "Bill the Cat".

But, yes, it can get worse, by a lot. Suppose you find out that you actually have more than one thing you need Joe to do for you. You really have 5 things. That means that all the integration work you just did with Joe for that one little tiny functional thing just got blown up into something that's 5 times as big. And, Joe can't do thing number 4 until his buddy Sam (who you never cared for, anyway) does something for HIM. You have a dependency on Joe, which creates a new dependency on Sam. You now have a *dependency chain* at work, which is a risk to your plan. And maybe you can coerce Joe into doing what you need on a particular schedule, but no way is Sam going to pay you any attention because of all those things you said about him back in third grade. Now you have to find a way to blend some of your rules with Sam's rules, which creates a vision in your head of snowballs in hot places. You've just lost control of your project.

What to do? You've gone to Sam to talk about this, and you've gotten a lot of "What? Can't hear you..." kinds of responses. And Joe has this look on his face, like "Can't blame ME, I tried", and that goes along with lots of shoulder shrugging. So, you go to Sam's manager to whine about this, and he says "I have dozens of other PMs whining at me about things, what makes your whine so special". Like that.

You're stuck.

But, you aren't the only PM who's ever gotten stuck like this. Organizations have seen this kind of thing happen before, and have slowly but slowly come to realize that they can't operate like that, because they actually have to get things *done*. It just doesn't pay to have people stuck all over the place. So, they've had to define a new set of rules, which you and all the other sad sack PMs get to blend in with all your own rules, to keep you all from getting stuck again. And, yea verily, these new rules were called "Teflon", because PMs by definition live in scalding frying pans, and need a way to keep from sticking to the sides when the heat gets turned up.

This is how we got things like "process" and "portfolio management" and "resource allocations" and all that. And, while you have been going merrily along with your PM blinders on, just worrying about your own little project sphere of happy times, somebody has to worry about how to get all you PMs to work together and keep your projects moving forward, because the business will cease to exist if that doesn't happen. Someone, who can actually provide you with support and the ability to resolve contentious problems with other teams, who can set the priorities for your organization, and can make sure that you have (almost) whatever you need to get your project done, that special someone needs to exist as the referee and quartermaster and den mother and ultimate supreme court justice of your organization. None of which you can do alone.

Thus... management.

You see,

Major CS+PM point: *No project is an island unto itself.*

You may think that your blinders protect you from having to worry about things going on in other projects, but that's not quite true. Go back to the chapter "What IS Project Management". Remember the point about resource contention, and how project management can be a way to manage that. Everything you commandeer onto your project, from hardware to money to intellectual property to people, all those things are resources of one type or another. And as "resources", they are finite. It's your job as PM to get access to them. It's management's job to prevent that. NO, that's not right. It might seem that way sometimes, but only in your universe. In their universe, management has to worry about ALL the PMs who want to get access to the organization's set of finite resources, so it's up to management to manage that access. Or, shall we say, *arrange* access to those resources. For a small fee, perhaps.

The actuality of this is that when the PMs pile inside the octagon to do battle for the unbelievably finite set of project resources, it's the not-PMs, a.k.a., the management types, who have to keep order in the ring to preserve life and limb. This type of competition breeds all manner of politics (see also: Socialism), and people get quite ingenious in figuring out ways to get around all the red tape that the process puts in their way. That works, sometimes. Not normally, because the gatekeepers to the resources you need have seen it all before, because they've *done* it all before, and they know how to keep their gates closed. Especially to keep *you* away from their stash. But, there are times when a certifiable crisis does arise, and you need special help to get your project ship back on the surface of the pond again, and these people will turn out to be your bestest buddies of forever when they help you. Don't forget that. Put them on your Christmas card list, because you *will* need their help again, and subtle gestures of appreciation can work miracles. And never let them find out that you manufactured that oh-so-important crisis out of whole cloth, just to get around the bureaucracy, because these folks have memories that would put an elephant to shame. You don't want to find out that their middle name is decidedly *not* "Forgiveness".

Remember the Orwellian reference to PMs being more equal than others? In your universe, just continue that line of Newspeak, and repeat after me: *managers are your friends*. Rinse and repeat.

Requirements

Here's a true story: during a customer briefing, it came time for the development executive to give his presentation. He walked up to the front of the room, and sat on the front edge of the table there. He crossed his ankles, then crossed his arms, and looked out at all the customer people in the audience. Then he said this:

"One thing I've learned over the years is that customers are inveterate liars."

Then he looked at the customers, sitting there, with stunned looks on their faces. And he let the silence linger for a while.

When he figured he had their attention, he said "What I mean by that is that at the beginning of a project, you tell us what your requirements are. Then, we go off and do the implementation and testing for them. Lots of effort in that. And when we're done with the work, we come back to you and have a review of what was done. And you say, but *that's* not what I wanted."

Aside from getting a chance to pontificate a little, he was making three points here:

1) You can't have vague requirements when you're starting a project. That leads to bad implementations which either miss important things or build things in the wrong way. And then scope creep happens because people figure that, what the heck, since we need to fix all the things which we missed when defining the requirements in the first place, adding a few new things won't hurt anyone.

2) You need to keep the customer in the loop about the state of the work all the way through the schedule, so that they're aware of what's being done and can have a chance to input about that, which is only fair since *they're paying for it*.

3) This is why contracts need to be in place which spell out in no uncertain terms what the requirements are, and what the costs are for changing them or adding new ones. You might conclude that contracts prevent lying, but don't forget that we're dealing with lawyers here, too.

This might have been an unorthodox way to get a point across, but he did get it across. And it was this:

Major CS+PM Point: *The first rule of everything is to understand the requirements before you start doing anything.*

Requirements tend to be a little squishy and imprecise. They get further refined in doing the architecture, and then again during the design phase, and maybe even once more when doing the development. But the further to the right you get when doing an implementation, the more expensive it gets to change a requirement. Changing or adding a requirement means you probably have to rip out some work you've already completed, which causes lots of tendrils of rework to be needed. If you're in development and you change a requirement, you may have to retool your architecture and update your design, and that can create a wide spread of impact to your development work. But if you find that a requirement has to be changed and you're still doing the architecture, well, heck, that just means you have to move a function block around on a piece of paper a little, and maybe add a new one someplace convenient, and you're done. Right? Right?

Of course, the situation is that you probably think you already *do* understand the requirements when you start doing project work, and it isn't until sometime down the road that you start to wonder, "just what the heck are we doing here", and realize that you really don't know what you were supposed to deliver in the first place. So, you've been wandering in the desert of self-complacency for a long time now, going along thinking that the direction you've been on has been just dandy, thank you very much. And then... something breaks and that shows you how silly you've been, thinking that you knew where you were going. Keep those plates spinning.

What you're seeing is that requirements are part of every stage of the project lifecycle. It doesn't matter if you're doing a software development project, or a consulting or services project, or any other kind of project. People tend to think that requirements are defined at the beginning of a project, when the project manager gets the Charter. And that's true, but only to a certain level, which for the requirements you get in the Charter, is around 100,000 feet.

The PMBOK says that in the Charter, you'll get a description of the problem being addressed, team members, budgets, various other things, and then a list of "high level requirements". These are all the things that the various project stakeholders want implemented. Typically, these are at a "business" level, because by and large, stakeholders have brains that they believe think in those terms. Let us not forget that the pesky things that flow out of business requirements, like technology requirements, are trivial details by comparison. You, as the project manager, have the job of translating these into sets of things your team can actually work with.

Suppose, for instance, that we go back to the example of our poor little engine bolt. The objective of our project is to build one. One of the requirements for the bolt is stated like this:

The bolt must be strong enough to resist the forces of the engine running so that the engine is kept from flying through the hood of the car.

Note the difference here between a "requirement" and an "objective". A project objective might be defined to say "The objective of this project is to build a bolt to hold the car's engine in place." But, that isn't really specific enough to be a *requirement*, so the objective has to be expanded to incorporate some more granular details about the bolt, like it's strength characteristics. And the requirement about it being "strong enough to resist the forces..." is the result.

But that's not enough to actually work with, either. So, this requirement needs to be expanded, too, so that more is defined about what it means to be strong enough. For instance, it could be said that the material the bolt was made from had to have a tensile strength of 250 MPa (MPa is MegaPascals... which sure clears THAT up. And, yes, I had to look that up[52].) And then you have to define other characteristics of the material, like its impact strength, stress-strain elasticity, deflection magnitude, and a whole lot of other things that may have equivalents in the English language. But when you're done with all that, you have a fully defined set of requirements for the material that need to be used in the manufacture of that bolt. But you still aren't done, because now you need to put the recipe together to blend all the constituent compounds that make up this bolt material, and then you have to define how to test it to make sure you got it all right, and then... and then... well, these things go on and on.

What you're seeing is that for every step along the left to right path you're taking to build your little bolt, each step has its own set of requirements, which are a stepwise expansion of the requirements from a previous phase. You get your business requirements in your Charter (or what passes for a Charter since not all organizations have actually heard of a Project Charter. What you get is actually a *metaphor* for a real Charter...) And those business requirements are

---

[52] That is 2 sentences in a row which end with the words "that up". Where else could you find that except in a book about project management?

used in the architecture phase to understand how that needs to be done. And part of the architecture phase is to define the design requirements, and the design phase defines the development requirements, and the development phase defines the test requirements, and so on. What you're left with is a huge spaghetti bowl of requirements. You as the PM have to sort those all out and make sense of them.

There are some requirements which encompass sufficient scope that they will actually be incorporated into *milestones*. You know the "what" part of the milestone, because that's what the requirement defines. But there are also implicit requirements which need to be factored into the milestones, too, like "who" will work on it, and "how long" it will take to complete. But, there are even more requirements built into *these* requirements. For instance, "who" implies "how much" because labor cost is associated with every "who". And if you have to go out and buy 30 tons of tungsten for your next manufacturing run of engine bolts, well, tungsten isn't free, you know. You have to account for its cost in your budget, and that is a requirement, too. There are requirements attached to every tangible thing you need to have in your project plan.

Of course, when we talk about "requirements" in a project sense, we don't normally include things like material or labor costs in that. Sure, those are part of the budget which is part of your plan, but they aren't considered to be "requirements" as such. Requirements normally go back to the definition of a project, and are defined to be things that specify the "unique product, service, or result" that your project is about. But we need to realize that anything which tells us *what* or *when* or *how* to deliver something in a project is a requirement. There may be functional requirements, or business requirements, or test requirements, or performance requirements, or usability requirements, or availability requirements, or any of a thousand other types of requirements. But they're all requirements. And as the PM, you need to understand ALL of them so that you can know which to include in your project plan to drive the team with, and which you don't.

And here's the stinker in all this... we all think that requirements are static, which of course, they aren't. But we like to think that once we have them defined, well, that's it, let's go build this puppy. Oh, what a rude world it is.

The fallacy in this line of thought is that when you go into a new phase of your project, you might discover that, *oops*, you forgot to account for something earlier in your planning work. And now you have to jam it into your plan. That forgotten thing might be a functional requirement, which you didn't actually forget about, but you just might have *not realized* it was needed because you hadn't gotten into the level of work definition where it was obvious that it was really, truly needed. Or, it might be a performance requirement, because the team didn't know when it was designing this thing that adding a hundred more users might have an actual impact on the network bandwidth, and now you have to scrounge more of that up someplace. Or, it turns out that the customer isn't too happy with the idea of their application crapping out on them every time a table in the database overflows, because, you know, that costs the business *real money*, which isn't great. All these things represent new requirements of one sort or another.

You might think that this is an opportune time to make one of two statements about this:

1) Your doofus team should have done a heck of a lot better job of making sure the requirements for all phases of the project were completely defined correctly from the get go. Or,

2) Of *course* it's impossible to know all of the requirements right from the beginning, because you haven't gone through enough work to have tripped over all the little rocks and tree stumps in your way to know what there is to discover out there that can break your plan into little tiny pieces.

And I would grade these statements as follows: 1) *Fail*. It is humanly impossible to know ahead of time what all the requirements are for all project phases. And, 2) *Fail*. You can't go into a project with the expectation that you'll be defining requirements along the entire project timeline because that would create a huge amount of rework.

I *told* you that requirements were squishy.

This is where all the Agileophiles get their knickers in a twist about *iterative development*. Let me just say a thing or two about that.

If you're in a research environment, and you have oodles of time to implement something, and you have lots of spare resources laying around the shop that you can pick and choose from to do that, and you don't really know what you're supposed to be implementing but your management is OK with paying you to fidoodle around in your little sandbox for a living, then Welcome to Nirvana. You have arrived.

But if you happen to exist in the *real world*, then you need to go about things a little more efficiently.

It's true that you can learn a lot about what work needs to be done from the lessons you learned in doing work in a previous phase. And, yes, it's a fallacy to think that you can create one giant monolithic implementation all at once and have it be correct. Verification steps like testing are natural feedback loops that will show you what you missed, and you may end up having to re-implement something in a different way as a result of something you "discover" during test. But it's just as much of a fallacy to think that you can go into a major implementation without first knowing very well what you're supposed to be developing.

This is not to say that prototyping is a bad way to discover things like functional requirements. If you're not really certain about what a product needs to contain or how it needs to work, try a part of it out and see what happens. Take that to a set of potential users to get their feedback about what works and what doesn't. Toss it if it doesn't work, and try something else. This is all cool, if you have that kind of time. But when you do that, just realize that prototyping puts you in a phase of your implementation which is more toward the right of your timeline than you want to be when defining requirements. And trying something out and then tossing it gets real expensive in a hurry.

What is more effective is to work with lots of potential users up front. Go through all the usage scenarios you can think of with them, and then smooth all the results of that out into a set of requirements for the product you want to develop. Depending on what scale we're talking about, those users could be part of an industry user group, or a set of well-known customers, or an ad-hoc brown bag research lunch group. But whatever scale it is, talk with the users first and get their ideas. Test those ideas out, again and again, with different groups. They will eventually coalesce into a set of requirements for the next version of your favorite product. Sure, even when you get to development for those requirements, you're going to run into some bumps along the way that will make you do rework. But they will most likely be minimal compared to the experimentation method of trying and tossing prototypes.

I had a situation in a group once where my technical lead decided he wanted to develop this cool new thing. It sounded really good, and it was obvious that, if he could pull it off, it would be incredibly useful to lots of folks. But, when I asked him to put a plan in place to define a box around it so I could sell it to management, he said "No," because it was really a research project where the requirements for capabilities of the product weren't known ahead of time, and they had to be "discovered" along the development path. I said, "OK, let's run with that for a while, but not forever." And every so often, he'd come up with a chunk of new parts for the product, and would show them off to the team, and they were great, no doubt. Very well done. But when I asked him how many more things was he planning on developing, he said, "I don't know, I haven't discovered everything yet." That was a very hard case to sell to the business because there were no bounds to it. There was no timeline for the work, no estimate of expenses, and no real definition of what function would be included. Clearly, the idea was a good one, and a product along those lines would be a real success. But it was an amorphous, undefined, unending effort, and that was a no-no for management. It would have been a lot easier sell if the requirements being satisfied were known at the beginning.

I have to admit, I've worked with many different development groups over the years, and there have been many times when they decided to build a product with a particular set of functions in them, and I have no idea where those requirements came from. Some of these features continue to exist for a long, long time, and you have to believe that their utility is way past. Like, the CAPS LOCK key on your keyboard. That is my favorite pet peeve. Why is that still there? I'm convinced that the only reason why the CAPS LOCK key still exists is that some ancient keyboard developer was a typing tutor in a past life, and he felt the need to punish you when you overshoot the "a" key with your pinky. After missing that a few times ND TYPING IN ALL CAPS UNTIL

YOU REALIZE WHAT HAPPENED, you want to get a pair of pliers and pull the damn key out.

There is something else associated with requirements that might not be as obvious, though, and that is *discipline*.

Major CS+PM Point: *Requirements exert discipline on a project.*

Things (supposedly) only get developed which satisfy a requirement. No scope creep here, please. Just develop what the requirements call for, and don't add a bunch of spurious feechurs.

This is critically important when you're working under the context of a contract, because this stuff called *money* is involved.

And to make a good contract work, it's critical to have the deliverables defined precisely. And the deliverables are the requirements of the contract (along with payment schedules and other trivialities).

Let's suppose, for example, that you're working on a contract to build the spaceship that will take all those people on the one-way trip to Mars that is all the vogue in certain circles right now. There are, obviously, enough requirements in that to keep you busy for quite a while. But, suppose you decide that going to Mars is nice, but *wow, would it be cool to go to Alpha Centauri first*. Heck, it's only a difference of

20 x 10**12 miles, and what's a few light years among friends?

That would not fly, so to speak.

On a more, well... *pragmatic* level, though, suppose you're in the middle of a project to build a new data center. You've gone through all the analysis to arrive at a specification of how many systems need to be in there, and how much networking is needed to support them, and how much air conditioning is needed, and power, and all the rest. These are all the project requirements. But, halfway through the project, you find out that, *wait*, there needs to be twice the number of systems in the center, and that means your air conditioning system is undersized, and your power supply is, too, and your floor can't hold all that extra weight, and... and everything. You have two options here:

1) Figure out what it would take to accommodate all the extra equipment in your work, and delay the project by that amount of time. Of course, there's an increase in budget that goes hand in hand with that, so you need to go to the management team and cry about that and get more precious funding allocated. And they need to approve your new schedule. And you get lots of lashes with many forms of wet pasta in the process. Or,

2) There is no second option.

This is the phase of the project which is called "Well And Truly Screwed". Not "Happy Times".

You might think this is an extreme example, and that no project team would be caught with their shorts down like this by not knowing the server requirements for the new data center ahead of time. But... you could well be wrong about that. Oh, yes.

A more likely example, though, is that you're in the middle of the data center project, and the customer comes to you and says "Hey, wouldn't it be great if we could stick this *other* server in the center, too. You know, the one that does payroll. Oh, sure, there's some SAN that goes along with that, and some new security things we'd need to do. But wouldn't it be *great* to do that?" And you'd say "But that's not in the contract," and the customer would say "Oh, let's not quibble about things..."

THAT is not just a fictitious example of scope creep. No no.

So, how should you react to that? Of course, you want to keep the customer happy about things, so you want to be as accommodating as possible. But here's where the discipline of requirements comes to your aid.

The right thing to do is to say "Well, we can't just add a new server that isn't in the contract. Either we need to modify the contract to include that, or we need to put a follow-on contract in place to handle it."

Why would you do that instead of just adding that one little server to the center, which would keep your very very important customer so happy?

Answer: *money*.

Along with requirements, every tangible thing in a project has a cost associated with it, and all those costs are defined in the contract. To add that new server, you'd have to architect it, and then go buy it, and then have someone install it, and then maintain it, and... lots of other things. And every single one of those things requires funding. And if you want your business to continue breathing, you can't just give money away, which is what you'd be doing if you did that kind of work outside the scope of the contract.

But, suppose the customer comes to you and says "Hey, about that data center... you know how we said that it needed to be done by December? Well, we really need it done by August, instead. Any problems with that?"

Oh, there might be just a problem or two with that.

You may have heard the term "crashing the schedule". There's a reason why it's called that. It means that you can throw more people on a project to accelerate a schedule (or, more likely, to keep it on track). But there are a slew of problems with that approach, like there may not be enough people available to crash with, or the people who are available may not have the right skills, which is probably why they're available in the first place.

But a major problem with this approach is that, if you do happen to hit the lottery and find enough people with the right skills to put on the project, there will be an onboarding period of time when they're getting familiar with all the ins and outs of the project, so it will take a lot of time away from the people already on the project to bring the new folks up to speed about things. And the more people there are, the more communication points there are, and remember what we said about the whisper game back in the chapter on Faith.

The net of this is that by bringing lots of new people onto the project, you've created an environment with a significantly increased amount of risk, and an enhanced probability of breakage.

Thus, I bring you... "crash". As in, "and burn".

But you could have avoided all this unpleasantness if you'd only relied on the discipline that requirements can bring you.

Here, let me help you out. There's a phrase you can use when a customer asks you to do something silly like accelerate a schedule, and it happens to be outside the scope of the contract. You can say this: *No*. OK, let's repeat that together: *No*. Good!

That, by the way, is actually being responsive to the needs of the customer. Why? Because *customers need discipline, too*. And that comes from adhering to the contract. If something needs to be done which is outside the scope of the contract, then use the change management process to get the contract updated, or put a new one in place to handle that. But don't just agree to doing something because the customer is ~~yelling at~~ begging you to do it. You won't have to worry about having too many customers in the future if you do that.

Look at it this way: if you don't say *No*, aside from all the discussions you'd get into with the nice legal teams, you'd be giving your services away for free. Now, do you think you could walk into Home Depot and say to them "You know, I really like that hammer over there. Would there be any problem with me taking it without paying for it? I really need something to hit myself over the head with from time to time, and that would work so well..."

Yes, yes, there would be a small problem with that, which could take you 5 to 10 years in your local State-sponsored spa to fix. So, how is giving your very valuable services away for free any different? It isn't.

See, requirements mean lots of different things. It's not just a matter of understanding what type of widget you have to build and when you have to deliver it. It's who's paying you, and how much, and specifically what for. There are business requirements, and functional requirements, and expense / capital requirements, and usability requirements, and performance requirements. Make sure they're all specified in the contract and kept up to date.

And, don't forget about requirements discipline. If you do, then open wide and get ready to swallow all the great scope creep coming at you, which you will end up implementing *gratis*. Wouldn't that be *great*?

PMeontology

"40 is the old age of youth. 50 is the youth of old age". So said Victor Hugo.

But, in high tech, our buddy Victor was a little off. There's a saying about aging in the high tech industry which goes like this:

"In high tech, if you're 30, you don't exist. If you're 40, you haven't existed for 10 years. And if you're 50, even your kids don't exist." Obviously written by someone who was not yet unextant.

But the salient attitude of high tech toward "experienced people" was captured succinctly by the Head Honcho of Ageism himself, Mark Zuckerberg, when he said "Young people are just smarter" to an audience at Stanford University. It was like, *everyone knows that*. He was at the ripe old age of 23 when he said that. And he was worth $1.5 billion (BILLION) at the time. Money talks, bull$#!+ walks.

There is some truth to the notion that the most *valuable thought* comes at an early age. Zuckerberg did co-found Facebook when he was only 19. Bill Gates co-founded Microsoft when he was 20. Steve Jobs co-founded Apple at 21. Orson Wells performed his "War of the Worlds" at 23. Michelangelo carved the Pieta at 24. Ernest Hemingway wrote "The Sun Also Rises" at 27. Mozart composed his first opera at 11. (That's "11", as in, "one year more than 10".) History is replete with people who achieved historic things at a very young age.

We have a phrase for these kinds of people: *freaks*.

It's one of history's odd coincidences that this word rhymes with "geeks".

But what does this all mean for project managers?

Well, let me ask... how many 22-year old project managers do you know?

Answer: Not one.

Why not?

Let's assume for the sake of discussion that a "project manager" is someone who has been granted the PMI certification of PMP. This is not a trivial thing to earn. In particular, if you have a 4-year degree, you need at least 4,500 hours of project management experience within the last 3 years to qualify as a PMP. But the assumption built into that is that you are in a job that will give you the chance to accumulate that many hours as a PM. And the reality is that you won't get that kind of a job unless you are already very experienced in a domain area where PM skills are needed. This is the paradox of project management:

> **Major CS+PM Point:** *You can't get certified as a project manager unless you have already been a project manager for a long time.*

This isn't a chicken-and-egg kind of question. We know what comes first: you have to *be* a project manager before you can be *certified* as a project manager. It sounds like a conflict in logic, but we *are* talking about project management here.

So, you can't just be born as a project manager. You have to *learn* how to be one, and that takes a fair amount of time. Now, add that to the amount of time it takes to learn enough about a particular domain area so that you get put in a position of actually managing things across your team, and you have a substantial time element for your PMP over and above just the certification process itself.

Suppose you're a UNIX systems administrator. That normally requires a 4-year degree, and training in a specific operating system area, and more training in a set of specific tools that you need to use to administer that system. It could take you a good 5 years or more to become proficient as a sys admin. But, to grow that into being a PM, you'd need to be so good at it that you start defining how other folks on your team would need to administer their systems, too, and eventually you might make it to a team lead position. That could take another 5 years, because there are lots of new skills you have to "learn by doing" when it comes to managing the work of other people. Let's say that in round numbers, you're 30 years old by the time you're ready to start your certification process to become a project manager.

30 years old? Heck, that puts you past the age of valuable thought, doesn't it? Jiminy Crickets, you mean you have to be over the hill to be a project manager?

Well, the story is even more harsh than that. ZDNet did a study[53] which showed that the average age of a project manager is 42. But the story is even more harsh than *that*. See, there are two types of project managers: 1) young ones, typically under 30, who have chosen project management as a career; and 2) older ones, who are "accidental" project managers, and who just happened to trip into project management as a job (versus a "career", a major distinction). And who, by the way, are in their early 50s.

---

[53] http://www.zdnet.com/project-managers-staring-into-generation-gap-1139251366/

And you thought the Hatfields and McCoys knew how to throw a party.

But this study is consistent with the two career paths of project management we discussed back in the chapter on Domain Expertise, those being technical and management. Think about it... as the ZDNet survey says, the younger PMs are more conversant with the technologies of the day, but lack the experience needed to form the kind of seasoned judgments required to be an effective PM. The older PMs have all kinds of that judgment-forming experience, but are pretty much stuck with the kind of technological expertise that lets you make tools out of stone. Or, punched cards. And the result of this dichotomy is that each camp thinks the other one is, to say the least, inept.

The PMI Annual Salary Survey[54] has a few other data points about this which are interesting, too. For instance, the percent of PMs in the US who have 20 or more years of overall *work* experience is 57 percent, but the percent who have 10 or less years of work experience is 11 percent. So, project managers tend to be well along in their careers, which means they're generally a lot older than the Zuckerberg

---

[54] It's here:
http://marketplace.pmi.org/Pages/ProductDetail.aspx?GMProduct=00101489101 . I tell you, this document is worth every penny of the PMI annual membership fee.

crowd. Interestingly, though, the percent of PMs who have 20 or more years of actual *project management* experience is only 16 percent, whereas the percent with 10 or less years is 41 percent. The inference from this is that most PMs are relatively new to the profession, irrespective of how long-in-the tooth they are otherwise. It's not too much of a leap to also infer that the younger PMs are specifically engaged in project management as a career, which is what the ZDNet survey says, as opposed to the older PMs who are doing it just for yucks. NO, they're doing it as a "career evolution", which means they kind of fell into it. Hidden in that, though, is the fact that the discipline called "project management" didn't exist when the older PMs first entered the workforce, so they had to pick up the credentials for it later on in their work lives, as opposed to having project management curricula laid out for them when they were in school. And, there are probably a lot of very experienced people doing the things that a project manager would do, but they aren't categorized into a job classification where they'd be called one. Overall, though, what this really means is that there is a distinct cultural divide between younger and older PMs. And that means there's friction between the groups.

This friction isn't just related to project management, of course. Society at large has this same schism between young and old. It's always been this way, but the world of high tech is evolving so quickly that this divide is not just more pronounced, it has much more significant cultural impacts across the generations, too.

Here's an example of that.

I went through the interview process for a PM position at a company involved in doing market research for web applications. There was a time when that was a pretty new age kind of thing for a company to be doing, but it had gotten to be fairly mainstream at the time. The recruiter I spoke with was real hot about my background and experiences, even more so than the normal slop these folks dish out. Then, I had the phone interview, and the vibes were real strong from that. I mean, the vibes were so strong, these folks just couldn't wait for me to get to their location for the onsite interview. So we set that up for the next week. I was scheduled to talk with a bunch of managers, and a couple of VPs, and of course, the "Big Guy" who ran the whole outfit.

When I got to their location, I was told that, oh, sorry, Big Buy can't talk with you today, he's too busy doing other stuff. OK, that sort of thing isn't uncommon. I went through the discussions with all the other folks, and the vibes from them were really good. I thought, wow, this is a lock.

Then, I was in the office of the person I'd report to if I took this position, and we were having a great discussion about how things would work once I came onboard, and so on. Real positive. We were going over their internal plans and talking about suggestions to make things better and laughing and having just a great time. And there's a knock at the door. And who's there, but Big Guy. He sticks his head in the door and says to the person I'm talking with, "Hey, do you have that report about such-and-such that I could borrow?" And then he looked at me. And I could see him shake his head, almost imperceptibly. But it was there. And he took the document and left the office.

And then all discussion stopped, and I was walked right out the front door, with a "We'll be in touch". And I never heard from them again.

What happened?

Well... I will be open about not being in the "inexperienced" group of PMs. I've been around a long time, and have seen it all at one time or another. All the problems and frustrations I've run into over the years are clearly written on my weathered face. Big Guy was young enough to be one of my kids. And when he looked at me, he must have seen what he thought was *dinosaurus obsoletus*, because to him, older people are obviously obsolete, and aren't worth hiring. So, the interview was then *over*.

Was that discriminatory? You betcha. But ageism is alive and well in high tech. It is so much a part of the foundation of the technology industry that it's like it was never any other way. There are no ancient and venerable masters in high tech. There are only young studs and more young studs. Read this article[55] to see how blatant age discrimination is.

So, what to do about it?

Hey, I could color my hair! That would make me look younger. But then I'd have to get a hair transplant to have something to color.

Maybe I could go with the flow and just shave my head to clear off the last remaining bits of moss. But I don't want to look like an escapee from the local light bulb factory. Speaking of which, I used to be the paperboy for a genial fellow named Gordon Liddy. (Yes, THAT Gordon Liddy.) Back then, he had a wonderfully full head. Of hair, I should say. Not sure what the rest of his head was full of. Anyway, he needed to take a sabbatical for a few years in the Danbury Home for Wayward Malcontents and Other Fallen Angels. After that, he decided to change careers (a good idea) and went into political punditry. Who better? Part of his reclamation story is that he evidently thought his makeover required a shaved

---

[55] http://www.newrepublic.com/article/117088/silicons-valleys-brutal-ageism

head, which he did. But I can't help thinking he looked like something that fell out of a pin ball machine, and I don't want to look like that. Having the perfect face for radio, as it were, I have enough strikes against me ever appearing in GQ as it is.

The truth is that there is nothing you can do to overcome this ageist mentality. It is what it is. And project management is a uniquely bad area for it, because it takes so long to get to be a PM. Almost by definition, if you're a PM, you're well past the curve of technical relevancy, according to the Zuckerbergs of the world. This is not so true in other industries, but high tech has this particular affliction that young folks don't need to know about, or care about, the history of their profession. And no one who has ever seen a punched card knows anything at all about modern technologies and all that webery stuff. I mean, come on, what's the average age of the people you see in a hackathon? I'll give you a hint: it's somewhere between 23 and 23.

And this is why this chapter is titled "PMenontology". That's right, the "study of high tech fossils". There is no "with age comes wisdom" philosophy here. No no. It's "with age comes obsolescence." It's no different than previous generations. It's just happening faster now, because technology is evolving so quickly. And, I have to say, I love it when I see the 30-year olds looking over their shoulder at the web kiddies crawling up *their* backside.

But, not to worry. I have seen projects staffed with inexperienced and unskilled people, all in the throes of cost management, and they universally come back to bite the organization in the *derrière*. There are no two ways around it...

Major CS+PM Point: *To manage projects effectively, you need a significant base of experiences that give you the judgment to know what works and what doesn't.*

And you only get that from having failed at something, and then figuring out how to keep going. That isn't something that you learn in school, or are given as an entitlement. No, no.

Major CS+PM Point: *Failure is a great teacher. If you don't fail, you haven't extended yourself.*

Just make sure to learn from your failures so that you don't repeat them.

Decrankification

After reading that last chapter, it would be entirely understandable if you happened to be a little... *cranky*. The picture painted there was not one of happiness, fulfillment and light. It's time to see if I can decrankify you a little.

Things are changing in the world of project management. And as a PM, you need to know what those changes are and what they mean to you as a PM. And how to survive them. Survive, perchance to prosper. (I *knew* I could get another Shakespeare reference in here somehow. Of course, that brings us to yet another one... *To thine own self be true*... but, then we get back to that "despair" thing again...)

Before we go through these things, it's worthwhile to think about how we could indicate the importance these changes have for you as a project manager. I use a brand-new tool for that, called the

"Broomometer". The origin of that is this: one day, I was chatting with an immensely astute and powerful person in a group I was in, and I happened to mention to her that a mutual acquaintance of ours was about to leave the organization because, as he put it, "I'm tired of having the broomstick stuck up my a$$ so often." And this person I was speaking with said "Honey, he doesn't understand... we use so many broomsticks around here that we have our own *carpenter*."

As I said... astute.

Let's make this easy. We'll use the scale of 1 through 4 "broom sticks" to indicate the impact of a change to you, where 1 is "not much", to 4, which is "get out of Dodge right now." An example of this is:

Thing that changes: Witty description...

Broomometer rating:

This means that this thing that changed isn't that big a deal to you. But, if something were really, really bad for you, and it rates a 4 on the Broomometer scale, it would look like this:

Broomometer rating:

whereupon you would say, Check please!, because you are so *outta there*.

And, so, on to what's changing...

Demographics: As mentioned, the demographics of project management are changing, particularly as they relate to age. It may well be that there are the two groups of PMs described -- the intentional, younger ones, and the accidental, "seasoned" ones. But, it's like Mark Twain said, "Buy land, they're not making it any more". They're not making the older PMs any more, either.

Project management is becoming a more deliberate career choice. It will be less and less common that people just fall into it as their career progresses. Why? First, the discipline of project management has become more well defined, and frankly, more entrenched, in recent years. That means that project management as a career choice is more established than it used to be.

In "the old days", people did all the things that PMs do today, but those things weren't aggregated into a specific profession. There have been times when my cynical self has thought that all the things that people really hated, like working with details and logistics and organizational politics and finances and lack of authority but lots of responsibility ... all those things were pulled together into this mammoth penalty box called "project management", and certain people who were due for some long overdue retribution were blasphemed with the title of "project manager". Let the ecstasy begin.

Cynicism aside, that's obviously not what actually happened. *Obviously*. What did happen was that businesses recognized the need to have a single point of contact for these relatively short-term, well-defined efforts. After all, it's so much easier to have just one person to beat up than having to cycle through a whole, disorganized team to find a target. So, the anointee for this was the project manager, whose responsibility was to get the work done, on time, under budget, with high quality, and with no whining. What unfortunately transpired was that three out of those four objectives were most often satisfied. The fourth was the subject of the beatings. Scramble them up all you want. You never get all 4.

Now, to be able to keep all of your project plates spinning, while at the same time excelling at what is called "management mollification" and also "plan mitigation due to resource appropriation by projects which are higher priority than yours", you have to be fairly maze-bright in negotiating the ins and outs of dealing with all the groups across your organization. This takes... experience. You have to have scars on your forehead from beating your head against all the walls that exist between groups, which were put there to ward off any resource filching. (Not that you were going to *filch* anything. *Appropriate* does sound so much more businessly correct.) So you need to have the experience of building and cultivating relationships with all these groups so that you know what levers you can pull to get what you need out of them. Relationship management is key here. And that takes time to develop, and a lot of seasoning to know how to ~~manipulate~~ manage. So, this is a plus for older PMs.

Having said that, older PMs are aging out of the profession. The supply and demand of that should work in favor of these experienced people, and it sometimes does. But there's no way of getting around the fact that the proportion of younger versus older PMs is changing in favor of the younger ones. And that is changing the salinity of the water in the PM pool, which is changing the PM culture, too. It won't be long before the younger PMs have greater influence in defining what "project management" is than the PM pioneers have. In fact, that's already happening. As it should. Project management is becoming more of a deliberate profession as a result. And that will have an effect on older PMs, so long as they're still around.

Broomometer rating:

Work location: It's getting less and less common to work with an entire team in one location. More often, people exist in widely dispersed locations, for reasons ranging from the effects of a global economy, to the increase of people who work at home now. The MO for working is more the conference call than the actual meeting. This presents a layer of organizational logistics for the PM which can increase project time, complexity, and risk.

But, this isn't as much of an issue as it might be. People are getting more used to the dispersive nature of the work force. And, larger companies have historically had locations in many different places, so the logistics of working through multiple time zones and the inability to just walk over to someone's desk to ask a question are commonplace today. The calendar coordination involved still represents a layer of work that a PM doesn't want to have to deal with, but that's the reality of our existence.

Broomometer rating:

Workforce reductions: Having said that work location isn't a big Broomometer factor, reductions in the workforce are. This comes under the auspices of cost management as companies have offshored significant amounts of work to global locations with ostensibly cheaper labor costs. But that sometimes backfires.

I was part of such a backfire. I had joined a group which I didn't know was put in place because the company had gone overboard with its offshoring. In fact, the jobs for an entire organization of skilled American workers, including support and call center and project management functions, were all offshored in an ill-advised attempt to reduce costs. Some clients, and one very large healthcare organization in particular, had the entirety of their service delivery organization offshored as part of this. It turned out that the folks in the new location could handle the more granular work activities fairly well. But projects were slipping dramatically because there was little effective project management expertise there. So, the company was forced to bring the PM role back onshore, and I was brought in as one of the PMs. That was an expensive lesson to learn, both in terms of real money and in harming the relationship with many clients.

There are other aspects of reducing the workforce which can be detrimental to a PM as well. I was part of a group where some top technical people were laid off so that some less expensive people could be brought in. It turns out that one of the people who were let go was key to a system consolidation we were planning. When we got into the actual consolidation, a problem surfaced which the new person couldn't handle, and the consolidation had to be cancelled. That did not make the client happy. We went through two more iterations of this before the consolidation could finally be completed. Not to say anything bad about the new person, but the feeling was high on the team that if the more experienced person had not been let go, he would have been able to work through the issue and the consolidation could have been completed. This is a prime example of penny wise, pound foolish, and it caused me as the PM many headaches to resolve.

The fact is that there are cost pressures on companies today which are much more severe than in days past. Some of this is due to the incredibly rapid pace of technology evolution, which itself increases operational costs for companies as they respond to increased competitiveness and the need to reduce time to market for their products. These kinds of cost pressures lead companies to make bad decisions. The easiest poor decision to make is that people are just interchangeable cogs in the corporate wheel, and can be changed out like light bulbs whenever costs need to be cut. That is a very short-term view, and leads to an erosion of expertise that keeps you, as a PM, from staffing your projects with people who have the experience to do things right. The result is a growing portfolio of projects that start slipping and failing, and that gets really expensive in a hurry. And then more costs are being cut to try and recover from that, which leads to more projects getting into trouble. And more. And before you know it, your company goes belly up because it can't deliver projects any more. All because of misguided corporate cost cutting programs. This is a real killer for projects.

Broomometer rating:

Cloud Computing: If we're honest about the Cloud, we'd say that it's still a long way from being mainstream. Of course, that depends on what we mean when we say "cloud computing". Anything that is virtualized can be considered to be "in the cloud". It doesn't matter if it's servers, or storage, or data, or applications, they can all be in the Cloud. And, only parts of them can be in the Cloud, too. An organization doesn't have to put everything there.

But what we are seeing is that Enterprise Application environments are, by and large, not good candidates for the Cloud. That's not to say that these vendors don't have Cloud offerings. They do. But the effort to migrate an existing Enterprise-scale application environment like ERP to the Cloud is anything but trivial. When a company already has many billions of dollars invested in such an environment, including all the hardware, software, application configurations, process bulwarks, and all the rest, that is a strong disincentive to moving all that to some distant location where it's managed by a group of people whom you have no interaction with or control over. It's one thing to virtualize technology, but it's something else to virtualize people, which presents a set of risks (and control issues) to C-suite types that they will not buy into. And couple that with things like the valid concerns with performance, availability, security, and cost of internet access to your crown corporate information jewels, and it's not hard to understand the reluctance of most companies to fully embrace the Cloud. Until Cloud vendors can offer the same level of enterprise characteristics as having your own data center does, and in particular the same level of assured future continuity, the move to Cloud will be piecemeal.

What this means for project managers is that there will be an abundance of projects in the IT space for the foreseeable future. Not that there will be enough funding available to actually *do* these projects, but there they will be, stacking up like so much cordwood, just waiting for winter to arrive. Also, for the parts that are put into the Cloud, there will be differences in the scale of implementations, since all the systems management and configuration types of activities that are such a large part of a data center's daily life will be offloaded to the Cloud along with the infrastructure. That leaves the focus to be on the core competencies of the businesses, as manifested by business processes and home-grown applications.

Perhaps the most significant fallacy of the Cloud, though, is that it will save companies money, because they won't have to spend so much on establishing and maintaining their own data centers. You have to think about the business model for the Cloud vendors in this. They aren't giving Cloud space away for free. All that systems management and software currency and availability that you've come to know and love in your own data center will still need to go on in the Cloud. And while there's an economy of scale at work in the Cloud, there's a major profit motive at work, too, and that didn't exist in your own data center. It remains to be seen how well the economics of Cloud computing will work out for everyone aside from the Cloud vendors.

So, will the Cloud be a threat to project managers? Certainly, not if you're working for a Cloud vendor. There will be a TON of work there, especially during the growth phase of the industry. That may level off once Cloud reaches its saturation point, but that won't happen for a very long time, and Cloud acceptance may never happen in the areas that are most concerned with security of and availability to their data. I tend to think of mainframes here, which in reality are their own Cloud environments.

But there will be an erosion of data center investments over time, and that will have an impact on the IT segment of project management. The most likely scenario will be a continuing bump in the need for IT project managers for years to come, which will stabilize and start to decline in the commercial areas as they complete their transitions to the Cloud. How long that will take is anyone's guess. But it's not something that project managers need to worry about quite yet.

Broomometer rating:

Mainstreaming Project Management: You might think this would be the ultimate threat to you as a PM, but I beg to differ. It's like Security. I was involved in information security as a development manager in a prior life. Security was an emerging area of interest at the time. Not that it was an unknown requirement for corporate environments to be secure, but the techniques of assuring the security of data, networks, and general system integrity were not widely known outside a small community of security experts inside the government and some companies which worked with them. Today, security is all the rage, given the Edward Snowden fiasco, the NSA snooping on your private emails and cell phone calls, and all the hacking and network buggery that is such an intimate part of the Internet. But the thought with information security was that it would eventually leave the Ivory Tower of Research and DARPA and make its way into the normal technology discourse so that it would become commonplace. No longer would it be a special case type of mentality. Everyone would be aware of it. Practice safe computing.

That is what Project Management will be like, too. Today, it's a separate discipline, with it's own methodology and presence in Corporate America. But the value of Project Management is too high to be contained like that. We are seeing more and more people in areas outside of project management adopt techniques and the general rigor that make project management what it is. People are more aware of things that project management defines, things like the importance of scope management, control, schedules, constraints, and the like. Of course, people have always known the importance of these things, but it wasn't until the discipline of project management came about that they realized that it all had a name. Project managers will need to shift away from the specific responsibilities of managing projects and move more toward integration with the business towers that they support today. This doesn't mean that a decline in the importance of project management is in the future. To the contrary, the value of project management will be more widely recognized, and its tenets will be adopted by an increasingly larger audience. That means that project managers as a separate and distinct profession will most likely decline, but the art and craftsmanship of project management will live on in the areas which will increasingly adopt it. So, PMs may need to transform into more business-oriented roles. But that represents an organizational acceptance of project management itself, and a tremendous growth opportunity for the PMs of the future.

Broomometer rating: None!

How YOU can participate

It's not enough to just be a project manager. You want to tell people about it. You want to share your great experiences that can lead to knowledge for someone else in the PM community. Here's your chance to fulfill your dreams! At least, as far as being a PM goes.

If you have an experience you think could be useful to other PMs, especially ones that help illustrate the practical side of actually being a PM, drop me an email about it at csandpm@sailcreek.com . If I'm able to use it, I'll include it in my next book, and will put your name in BIG LETTERS right next to it so you can get PDU credit for it. And, I will (honestly) be eternally grateful, as will the other PMs who read about it, for your help and contribution to the profession.

Thanks! And I now return you to your regular programming...

Appendix A - Major CS+PM Points

Preface

*   *If it looks like a project, and swims like a project, and quacks like a project... it's a project.*

Introduction

*   *Newbies make lots of mistakes. Your success as a Project Manager depends on how quickly you can recover from them, and how soon you can stop making them. And that takes time, which you don't have a lot of, and some practical guidance, which this book provides.*

What's the point of this book?

- *Things aren't always what they appear to be, especially when it comes to defining what "project management" is.*
- *Wallflowers don't make good project managers.*
- *Project management is what <u>you</u> make it out to be as a project manager. If you don't define what it is, according to your perspectives and experience, someone else will do it for you. And you'll have to live with that, right or wrong.*

What IS "Project Management"?

- *Infinite requirements + finite resources = organizational contention.*
- *Project management is meant to help identify and manage requests for organizational resources.*
- *To be an effective project manager, you need to have these skills: 1) Discipline expertise; 2) Domain expertise; and 3) Leadership.*

Bullet 1: Discipline Expertise

- *If you don't follow the PM's Path To Enlightenment, then you WILL need to do a bunch of YOUR work over again.*
- *For any project effort today, you can't do it all alone. If you could, it wouldn't be a project.*

Bullet 2: Domain Expertise

- *Being a project manager means you have a very thin veneer of management skills that you can apply to something.*
- *To manage a project which delivers X, you need to know what X is.*

Bullet 3: Leadership

- *No matter how good your plan is, there is always room for things to go wrong. And they will.*
- *In project management, you want to be the composer, because that's where leadership is.*
- *Leadership is the ability to drive a group of people to a consensus agreement which supports your point of view.*
- *Treat people with respect and view them as the professionals that they are, and they will go the extra mile for you.*

Socialism

- *If you want to be an effective project manager, you need to be a good socialist first.*

- *It is in your own self-interest to treat your team with respect by appropriately recognizing a job well done.*
- *Risks are as much a part of project planning as accomplishments, so it's key to spread them around, too.*
- *Socializing accountability for resolving problems will go a long way toward making your life as a project manager more enjoyable.*

Faith

- *Faith is trusting that the people on your team really do know what they're talking about, and even if they stumble on things once in a while, that they'll keep at it until they get it right.*

ManageMental

- *There are different universes of thought to deal with when managing projects.*
- *No project is an island unto itself.*

Requirements

- *The first rule of everything is to understand the requirements before you start doing anything.*
- *Requirements exert discipline on a project.*

PMeontology

- *You can't get certified as a project manager unless you have already been a project manager for a long time.*

- *To manage projects effectively, you need a significant base of experiences that give you the judgment to know what works and what doesn't.*

- *Failure is a great teacher. If you don't fail, you haven't extended yourself.*

About the Author

DANA KILCREASE, PMP, lives with his wife and family in the beautiful Mid-Hudson Valley region of New York State. In addition to his "many" years of experience as a consultant in the technology industry, where he has managed countless data center implementations and business environment enhancements, he is also a voracious reader, a fingerstyle guitarist, and an avid golfer. And, alas... a technology junkie, too.

Two roads diverged in a wood, and I --
I took the one less traveled by,
And that has made all the difference.

Robert Frost, "The Road Not Taken", 1920

<<<◇>>>